I Want My Dinner Now!

Simple meals for busy cooks

Renee Pottle

Hestia's Hearth Publishing and Design * Kennewick, Washington

I Want My Dinner Now!

Simple Meals for Busy Cooks

By Renee Pottle

Published by:
Hestia's Hearth Publishing and Design
PO Box 7059
Kennewick, Washington 99336
www.hestiashearthpublishing.com

For additional copies of this book, please contact the publisher.

ISBN   0-9760137-1-1

First Edition

Library of Congress Control Number: 2004095535

Pottle, Renee

Cover Design by: Winsome Design, Inc. Richland Washington

Dedication

With love and gratitude to my husband, Stephen, who graciously supported my dream, tried every recipe without complaint, and gently prodded me along when I became stuck. Without him, this book would still be an idea.

About the Author

Renee Pottle is a Home Economist and freelance recipe developer. She also has a strong science background, and taught Food Science, Nutrition, and Health courses for many years. Renee developed the curriculum and taught the adult education class "Quick, Healthy, Budget-Friendly Meals" which was the basis for *I Want My Dinner Now!* Renee has always loved to cook, and has been creating new recipes since she was ten years old. She makes her home in Kennewick, Washington where she has two additional cookbooks scheduled to be published in 2005; Just a Little Bit Fancy: Saturday Night Suppers, and Cooking with Meat Substitutes. Both will be available from Hestia's Hearth Publishing and Design.

Acknowledgments

Writing a book is a fulfilling and sometimes overwhelming task, but definitely not one that can be done alone. I have been fortunate to be the recipient of help and advice from numerous people whose input has been invaluable.

My thanks go to Melissa O'Neil Perdue, Braiden Rex-Johnson, Sherri Schultz, Betsy Wray, and the staff at the Mid-Columbia Library - Kennewick branch - all of whom helped point me in the right direction while I was preparing this manuscript.

Thanks also go to Judith Dern and Andi Bidwell, who kindly poured over the recipes with a professional eye, identifying errors and ambiguous terms. To my mother, Greta Brown, my husband, Stephen Pottle, and my friend, Laurie Church who all contributed their favorite recipes, and to my sons, Adam and Trevor Pottle, who tried as many of the dishes as they possibly could.

Special thanks go to Jane Winslow and the staff of Winsome Design, to patient models N. Lee Prince, John Winslow, April Connors, Rob Dickson, Tracy Hill, Lafe Bissell, Reillee Williams, Justin Meyer, Cameron Winslow, Colin Dickson, and Emily Dickson, and to photographer Mark Roberts.

Table of Contents

About the Publisher

HESTIA'S HEARTH PUBLISHING AND DESIGN

In Greek mythology, Hestia was the first child of the old gods Cronus and Rhea, and sister to the powerful Zeus and Hera. As the goddess of the hearth and symbol of the home, she was the most sacred of the twelve great Olympian gods.

There are no tales of Hestia; as protectress of the household it was considered unseemly to gossip about her. Therefore, Hesia is seldom mentioned in English literature.

In ancient Greece however, each meal began and ended with a prayer to Hestia. The cities all had a public hearth where a perpetual flame burned in her honor. When colonists moved elsewhere, they carried a flame from the public hearth to protect their newly founded homes.

Here at Hestia's Hearth Publishing and Design we carry on the memory of Hestia by providing you with products that add beauty to your home, make it a little easier to manage, save you precious time, and make you smile.

Look for our new cookbooks; Cooking with Meat Substitutes and Just a Little Bit Fancy: Saturday Night Suppers, and the Kitchen Garden Quilt pattern collection, all coming in 2005.

Introduction

When did our lives start moving at warp speed? It seemingly happened overnight. One day we were calmly moving along in a horse and buggy world, and the next morning, like Rip Van Winkle, we woke up to a world filled with modern technology. Now we seem to be stuck on fast forward. There are just not enough hours in the day to get everything done. And almost all of us suffer from this lack of time; single college students trying to make ends meet while studying and holding down a part-time job, young families with "two jobs, two cars, two kids, a cat and a dog", single parents trying to go to work, clean the house, do the laundry, and read to the kids, and middle-aged career builders, juggling the needs of the workplace, older parents and young adult children at the same time. Whatever our situation, we can all use help finding good tasting food at an affordable price while saving us time too.

In response to this time squeeze, the traditional family dinner has flown out the window. Who has time to prepare a home cooked meal, and then the energy to clean up afterwards? Grocery shopping has become a chore often done each night on the way home from work, buying what we need just for that evening. More often we avoid cooking altogether and run to the nearest fast food place for dinner. Follow this practice too many nights and our waistline grows as our wallet shrinks.

I Want My Dinner Now! solves this dilemma. This collection of 85 recipes is written with today's busy families in mind. The ingredients are easy to find, no matter where you live, and the directions are simple with few steps, even a novice cook can prepare a delicious meal. Most meals are prepared using few dishes to reduce the dirty dishes pile, and can either be fixed in advance or made quickly once you get home. Grocery and pantry lists are included for each recipe and suggested weekly menus start on page 139. The food included here is simple, but good and is designed to fit today's palates. You will find restaurant favorites made easily at home, like Sweet and Sour Chicken, Taco Salad, Chicken Cacciatore, and Vegetable Curry. Home-styled favorites, including Easy, Cheesy Mac, Better Than a Burger Meatloaf, Chili, and New England Fish Chowder are here, along with quick versions of traditionally labor intensive meals, Lasagna, Fancy Baked Beans, and Chicken Noodle Soup. And I scoured the family recipe files to choose the very best my family has to offer, my mother's specialties - Greta's Favorite Casserole and Mom's Ham Steak - Grammie Pottle's delicious Chicken and Rice Casserole, and my friend Laurie's Thai Chicken. You will also find some truly unique, kid-friendly meals, Turkey Wraps that include child favorites peanut butter and mandarin oranges, Easy Beef and Macaroni Pot, and Welsh Rarebit. Cooking dinner is not a science though, it is an art - experiment by adding your own style. You would have to work really hard to ruin a recipe. Be creative and add a few more vegetables, or substitute broccoli for green beans. The recipe calls for 2 cups of chicken but you have 2 1/4? Use it all. Use the recipes included here as a jumping off point to develop your own creations.

I Want My Dinner Now! has four main recipe sections. All four include a variety of family favorites, ethnic flavors, light meals and hearty fare. They have all been tested and approved by my

8

husband and sons - who don't hesitate to tell me when something doesn't work. All can be made quickly or easily, perfect for a busy weekday night.

Fast and Simple: Quick recipes that can be on the table in 35 minutes or less are the specialty here. Light meals with plenty of flavor, like Herbed Chicken Stir-Fry and Apple Sauced Pork Chops along with really quick dinners, Welsh Rarebit and Greek Frittata, and new twists on old favorites, Pizza Burgers and Fruity Chicken Salad.

Toss It In the Oven: Comfort food that cooks while you relax. It doesn't get any better. These favorites, including Scalloped Ham and Potatoes, Tamale Pie, Easy Cheese Mac, Lasagna and Better Than a Burger Meatloaf can be fixed quickly and then baked. The perfect meals for a stormy evening or a potluck dinner.

One-Pot Meals: I love to cook, but hate dirty dishes. Since I have never been able to afford a housekeeper, or talk anyone else into doing the dishes, I have spent years developing recipes that use very few pots and pans. The results, Skillet Chicken and Rice, Chef's Salad, Pasta with Fresh Mozzarella, Cauliflower Cheese Soup, and many others, are here.

Let's Use Those Appliances: We love our appliances. Most of us either own, or covet, a microwave oven, a blender, and electric grill, a pasta machine, a slow cooker - the list goes on. Here you will find recipes using four of the most common, and inexpensive, small appliances, the microwave oven, a rice cooker, a slow cooker and the newest star of the appliance world, the electric grill. The beauty of these tools is that you can basically throw all your ingredients together and let the appliances do the cooking. Try the unbelievably quick microwave Beef and Vegetables, or use your slow cooker to make a delicious Marinara Sauce. Let your teens make their own Veggie Quesadillas on the electric grill or try the unusual Orange Chicken and Spinach from your rice cooker. Let's take those appliances out from under the counter and use them.

My days are probably just like yours. They go by quickly, and I seem to add two things to my to-do list for every one thing I cross off. I love to cook, but don't always have the time to make fancy meals. This book is a compilation of my response to that problem. The meals are easy to prepare, but tasty and with lots of variety. They helped to relieve the stress of "what's for dinner" in my home. Although I cannot make life move more slowly for you, I do hope that *I Want My Dinner Now!* will help ease your race. If you desire more elaborate meals watch for "Just a Little Bit Fancy: Saturday Night Suppers" to be published by Hestia's Hearth in the fall of 2005.

The following product tips will help you have a delicious, budget friendly dinner on the table in record time:

> **Salt and Pepper**: Most recipes here do not include either salt or pepper, as some people prefer little seasoning, while others prefer a lot of seasoning. Please add both to fit your individual taste. This is also a good place to splurge a little - buy cracked black pepper and a gourmet salt. Both add much more flavor than the usual ground varieties, and you will actually use less.

Dried Seasoning: Wherever possible dried seasonings are used instead of fresh. Although we all love fresh seasonings, onions, garlic, and herbs don't keep well in the cupboard. Using dried seasonings helps save you money and time. If you are interested in drying your own seasonings, see the Basic Recipes section.

Packaged Food: Very little packaged food is included in the following recipes. But all have the ease of packaged food without the packaged taste. Most pre-packaged food includes large amounts of salt and other preservatives, which are not healthy for any of us and hide the real taste of good food. Using frozen and pre-cooked ingredients is a healthy way to get the fresh food taste with packaged ease. Many children are also sensitive to the preservatives found in packaged food, and should only be fed packaged foods in limited amounts.

Vegetables: Frozen vegetables are used more often than fresh, eliminating storage concerns. Frozen vegetables are more nutritious than canned, and often more nutritious than fresh vegetables that have been sitting in the refrigerator for a while. They also retain their fresh-like taste better than canned vegetables and can be stored easily for long periods of time.

Tomato Products: Many recipes call for small amounts of canned tomatoes, tomato sauce or tomato paste. Which leads to the question, what do

11

I do with the leftovers? I keep a "tomato" container in the freezer and just add leftover tomato products as I have them. Thawed, this tomato melange can be made into a delicious Marinara or pizza sauce.

Serving Size: All recipes included here are for 2 servings and 6 servings, perfect for a small family who doesn't need days of leftovers, or a larger family with hearty eaters. Need 3 or 4 servings? Simply halve the six servings or double the 2 servings.

Pantry List: Save yourself time by keeping a well stocked pantry. The pantry list on page 43 shows you what to keep on hand to easily make all these recipes.

Grocery List: Each recipe and weekly menu includes a list of items to buy from the grocers. Follow the list to make all the recipes quickly and reduce last minute buying.

Cook's Help: Suggestions to round out your meal, making it nutritious as well as deliciously attractive, are included with each recipe. Here are some additional tips to help you save time and prepare dinner with ease:

- Chop all ingredients before starting to cook.

- Place cut up ingredients in separate dishes and add each when called for, just like the TV cooking shows do.

- Do as much preparation the night before as possible.

- Read the entire recipe before starting to cook.

- Use pre-cooked, packaged chicken if saving time is more important to you than saving money.

- Cook a large amount of chicken at one time and freeze in individual packets to save money.

- Follow the weekly menus, taking the angst out of planning weekday meals.

Cook's Tips

■ Using frozen broccoli? Place it under running hot water for a few minutes to thaw. Or use fresh broccoli in any of the recipes here - just cook it in the microwave for a few minutes before adding to the recipe.

■ You can make your Paella (page 55) more authentic by adding a drained can of shrimp to the skillet.

■ Look for canned coconut milk in the ethnic foods section of your grocers. Don't confuse it with cream of coconut, which is used for beverages and desserts.

■ Make sure your skillet handle is oven proof before broiling the frittata (page 64) by covering it with aluminum foil.

■ Watching your cholesterol? Use ¼ cup of egg substitute for each egg in any of these recipes.

■ Rich, flavorful cheeses work best in a sauce. Use Cheddar, Feta, Gouda, Swiss or any other rich cheese. Avoid Mozzarella or provolone, as their delicate flavor is too mild for a white sauce.

COOKING BASICS
SAFETY

Did you know about one fifth of all home accidents occur in the kitchen? With all those knives, electric outlets, heat sources and more, the kitchen can be a very dangerous place. Most of these accidents are preventable however, with a little common sense. The following tips will help you keep your family safe from kitchen accidents and incidents, making meal time a memorable event for the right reasons.

Food poisoning occurs more often that we think. Many times that "24 hour flu bug"is really a case of food poisoning. Food poisoning in the extreme can be serious, particularly for children and is always unpleasant, whatever your age. To reduce your chances of food poisoning:

• Keep hot foods hot. Don't let food sit out at room temperature longer than two hours. Foods that are meant to be served hot (soups, hot entrees, etc.) should either be kept above 140° or be chilled. Bacteria grows rapidly at room temperature, but heat above 140° can kill the bacteria.

• Keep cold foods cold. Foods that are to be served cold (cream pies, sandwiches, etc.) should be kept at a temperature below 40° to prevent bacterial growth. Foods that need to be stored cold before preparing (meat, poultry, fish, eggs, cheese) should also be kept below 40°.

• Keeping your kitchen clean will prevent bacterial growth. Along with having clean work surfaces, when handling food, always wash your hands with hot, soapy water before touching food, and be sure your hands stay clean while preparing the meal. No playing with pets, fixing your hair, or coughing without washing your hands again.

• All utensils, cutting boards, and other implements used when handling raw meat should be washed before re-using. Never serve chicken or other foods from the grill in the same plate that you used to transport the raw ingredients without first washing with hot, soapy water.

Kitchen accidents are also common. The kitchen holds a lot of potentially dangerous equipment, it is usually a busy place, and family members have a tendency to congregate there, sometimes distracting us from what we are doing. To stay safe, follow these simple tips:

• Make sure that your hands are dry when using any electrical appliance. After each use, unplug countertop appliances. Never yank on the cord to unplug, but grasp the thick plastic end firmly where it fits into the socket.

• Use dry pot holders to handle hot pans. Wet pot holders can conduct the heat to your hand.

• Never try to catch a falling knife. Let it fall and then pick it up.

• Keep pot handles turned towards the center of the stove. Children are often severely burned by grabbing a pot handle and pulling the hot contents over on top of themselves.

• Use a stool to reach items on high shelves. Never climb onto the counter to reach something. It is too easy to lose your footing and fall.

• Don't place knives in a sink full of soapy water. Set them aside and wash one at a time. Or better yet, wash, dry, and put knives back in the knife block as soon as you've finished using them.

• Never wear loose clothing with sleeves or loose fabric that can dangle close to the stove. Fabric can catch fire easily.

MEASUREMENT EQUIVALENTS and ABBREVIATIONS

	EQUAL
1 ½ teaspoons	½ Tablespoon
3 teaspoons	1 Tablespoon
4 Tablespoons	¼ cup
5 ⅓ Tablespoons	⅓ cup
8 Tablespoons	½ cup
16 Tablespoons	1 cup
1 Tablespoon	½ fluid ounce
1 cup	8 fluid ounces
2 cups	1 pint
4 cups	1 quart
2 pints	1 quart
4 quarts	1 gallon
tsp.	teaspoon
Tbsp.	Tablespoon
oz.	ounce
lb.	pound

COOKING TERMS

- **Bake**: Baking is cooking foods in an oven at a constant temperature, and is the method of cooking most closely associated with warm memories of home and hearth. Many of our favorite foods are baked; decadent chocolate cake, soft molasses cookies, buttery biscuits, and home-styled casseroles. Baking is also an excellent way to warm the house on a cold or damp day, saving energy by fixing dinner.

- **Broil**: When an item is broiled, it is cooked by direct heat, under the heat source. Using a broiler pan, which is a two part pan consisting of a slotted top with a pan that fits underneath, is convenient, but not absolutely necessary to broil food. However, because you are cooking so close to the heat source, fatty foods may catch fire unless you are using a broiler pan. Foods are broiled anywhere from two to six inches from the heat source, but four inches will be adequate for most foods. Keep watch of your food when broiling so that it does not overcook.

- **Chop**: Chopping is cutting food into small pieces. There is some disagreement over what size pieces are when they are chopped. For the recipes in this book, I have used the term chop to identify pieces about one-half inch in size.

- **Crisp Tender**: A term predominately used when referring to vegetables. The vegetables are at the crisp-tender stage when they are cooked until slightly soft, but still crisp.

19

• **Dice:** Diced ingredients are cut into pieces ¼ inch or smaller.

• **Fry:** Frying is cooking food in a small amount of fat at a high temperature until brown and crisp. Deep-frying, the method of cooking so popular with fast food establishments, is cooking by submersing food into a pot of very hot oil or other fat. Deep frying requires additional attention to safety issues and adds many calories to the item you are cooking. Frying is a quicker, less messy way to seal in flavor, especially when cooking meats.

• **Grill:** Grilling is a similar process to broiling, using a gridiron or similar appliance and cooking over the heat source instead of under the heat source. Meats, fish, and vegetables can all be successfully grilled.

• **Sauté:** To sauté is to quickly cook or brown food in a small amount of fat. Sautéing brings out subtle flavors, especially in vegetables. Foods are best sautéed in a large skillet, and a heavy bottomed skillet will sauté foods better than a light weight skillet.

• **Simmer:** Simmered foods are cooked in a liquid kept just below the boiling point. Simmering helps to meld food flavorings.

• **Stir-fry:** Stir frying is a technique of cooking food in small amounts of hot fat while stirring constantly. It is traditionally an Asian method of cooking, but is now commonly used elsewhere. Although stir-frying is easiest when you have a wok, any large skillet can be used successfully.

HERBS AND SPICES

Herbs and spices, when used correctly, enhance the natural taste of food and have been used to do just that for centuries. Evidence has been discovered of the ancient Sumerians using thyme and laurel (bay). Herbal usage was also common in China as early as 2700 B.C.E. Spices have been so valued throughout history that they were once worth their weight in gold, and their lure launched numerous expeditions in search of new, more affordable producers.

Herbs are the flowers, leaves, stems and seeds of non-woody plants. Every culture seems to have its own favorite herbs. Italian cuisine is rife with oregano and basil dishes, mint and dill are common in Middle Eastern dishes, the French prefer tarragon and fennel, and traditional English dishes often use sage. Although herbs are most flavorful when fresh, unless you grow your own it can be difficult to find a steady supply. Dried herbs are adequate substitutes when using fresh herbs is impractical. Dried herbs will, however, gradually lose their flavor after about six months.

Spices are the dried flowers, bark, roots and leaves of mostly tropical plants. In the days before modern refrigeration, spices were used to mask the taste of meat that had been kept a little beyond its time. Spices were also used to preserve meat, making it into jerky, to be used at a later date. Spices are less delicate than herbs, and therefore keep their flavor longer. Even when spices begin to lose their flavor, you can simply add more than the recipe recommends.

• **Basil**: Basil is an herb, related to the mint family. It is used in tomato and egg dishes, soups and salads and is especially common in Mediterranean cooking. Fresh basil adds color and a rich, buttery flavor to foods. Dried basil is less flavorful than fresh, but still adds a nice summery taste to many dishes.

• **Bay Leaf**: Bay is the leaf of the Laurel tree. Ancient Greek heros were crowned with leaves of Bay, a tree native to the Mediterranean. Bay adds a complex, woodsy flavor to soups, meats and fish.

• **Cajun Seasoning**: A seasoning mix of the French-Southern style of cooking. Cajun seasoning can be found in the spice aisle of your grocers and usually includes a mixture of paprika, onion, pepper, salt, cumin and thyme in addition to other herbs.

• **Cayenne Pepper**: Cayenne pepper is the ground seeds of the hot, red pepper. Because it is such a hot spice, cayenne pepper should be used in small doses. It is also best when kept in the refrigerator to retain its flavor. Cayenne pepper is sometimes simply called ground red pepper.

• **Chili Powder**: Chili powder is another pre-mixed seasoning, used in many Mexican dishes. The mixture commonly includes chili pepper, cumin, and oregano. Chili powder is also best kept in the refrigerator to retain its flavor. Any chili powder mix labeled as "Mexican" is very hot.

• **Crushed Red Pepper**: Crushed red pepper, sometimes called chili flakes, are the seeds of mildly hot peppers. This is the pepper common in pizza parlors, available to add to your pizza or other tomato based sauces.

• **Curry Paste**: Curry paste is a paste made from fresh or dried chili peppers and other ingredients common in Indian and Thai dishes, like lemon grass, ginger and lime. This paste can be purchased in the ethnic food aisles of most grocery stores. It is available in red (very hot), green (quite hot) and yellow (still hot). A very little bit of curry paste goes a long way - so use it with caution.

• **Curry Powder**: In the far east, every good cook has their own secret curry recipe, usually a mixture of turmeric, fenugreek, anise, ginger and other spices. In the United States, curry powder is most often available as a sweet mixture, not a hot mixture - even when labeled as a hot curry powder - which is why I prefer to use curry paste. Curry powder is common in Indian and Thai cooking.

• **Ginger**: Ginger is the pungent root of a plant and can be used either fresh or dried and ground. Fresh ginger is often used in spicy Indian, Thai, and Middle Eastern dishes. Ground ginger is most common in the United States in baked goods, especially around the holidays. Ground ginger is an adequate substitute for fresh ginger, although it does lack some of the complex flavor of the fresh root. Candied ginger is a treat for all those who love the sharp taste of ginger.

• **Lemon Pepper**: Lemon pepper is another seasoning mixture, this of dried lemon peel and black pepper. Lemon pepper can be used for just about any meal, but is especially good with meat, egg and fish dishes. I also like to sprinkle it over fresh zucchini, which is then grilled.

• **Marjoram**: Sweet marjoram is one of many herbs belonging to the mint family. Although marjoram's taste is often compared to that of oregano, it offers a more complex, earthy flavor. Marjoram is especially good in soups, cheese, and vegetable dishes.

• **Mustard (Dry)**: Dry mustard is one of three forms of the popular pungent herb. Mustard is also available as seeds and prepared in numerous varieties, from sweet to hot. Dry mustard is made from the ground seed and is used to add zing to all dishes.

• **Oregano**: Oregano is relative of the marjoram plant, and like marjoram is commonly used in Mediterranean cooking. A stronger form of the herb is popular in traditional Mexican dishes, but because the two forms taste distinctly different, Mexican oregano should be used for Mexican dishes, and the more common oregano for Mediterranean based dishes. Oregano lends its unique taste to red pizza and pasta sauces.

• **Paprika**: Paprika is a red powder made from ground peppers. Most of us know paprika as the decorative red dusting on deviled eggs, but paprika is actually a very versatile spice, available in fiery hot to mild and sweet. Hungarian sweet paprika is the best, if you can find it at the grocers. It adds a deep, rich flavor to meat and fish dishes. Paprika, like cayenne pepper and chili powder, should be kept in the refrigerator to ensure freshness.

• **Thyme**: Thyme is another herb originally found in southern Europe, and is also a member of the mint family. Thyme's strong, sharp taste can be overpowering. It is best to use it in small amounts, and increase those amounts as you acquire a taste for the herb. Thyme is commonly used to flavor meat and poultry dishes, and hearty stews.

• **Turmeric**: Turmeric is a bright yellow spice, often referred to as "the poor man's saffron", as it is a cost effective substitute for the very pricy saffron. Turmeric adds color to curries and is also used in pickling.

INGREDIENTS: OTHER

The recipes in "I Want My Dinner Now!" use ingredients that may be unfamiliar to some of you. I have attempted to include a description of those items which are not commonly used by many cooks. Some of these ingredients add ethnic flair to your restaurant favorites, others are items that are available at most grocery stores, but you may have to dig a little to find them. All should be available - no matter where you live in the United States.

• **Bok Choy**: Bok Choy is a Chinese cabbage with thick white stalks and dark green leaves. It is sometimes called celery cabbage or Chinese chard, as it bears a resemblance to Swiss chard. Bok Choy is a versatile vegetable that can be sliced and steamed, and used as you would celery or spinach. It can be found in the produce section at your grocers.

• **Cellophane Noodles**: Cellophane noodles, also called bean thread noodles, are clear, thin noodles made from mung bean flour. Cellophane noodles are the Eastern Asian form of pasta. They can be easily cooked by soaking in hot water and then used in stir-fries. They can be found in either the ethnic food section or pasta section at your grocers.

• **Chutney**: Chutney is a highly seasoned, sweet-sour relish, commonly eaten with Indian and Thai dishes. The most widely known chutney is made from mango, spices and vinegar. However any fresh or dried fruit can be used to make chutney.

• **Coconut Milk**: Coconut milk is simply the liquid that results from grating coconut meat. Although purists agree that fresh coconut milk is the preferred form, luckily its canned version is readily available at the grocers. Coconut milk does not keep well after opening, and any leftovers should be frozen if you are not going to use them within one day. You will find canned coconut milk, and its low fat version, in the ethnic foods section of the grocers.

• **Cous Cous**: Cous cous is perhaps best known as a Moroccan dish, but is also common in other North African nations as well as the Middle East. Cous cous is actually very small grains of pasta, usually made from semolina but sometimes made from corn or barley. Cous cous can be served plain, or dressed up with spices and broth. Although you will find cous cous mixes in the grocery store along with the rice mixes, look for plain cous cous at your local health food store and add your own flavorings.

• **Egg Substitute**: During the 1980's, eggs became the *persona non grata* of the food world, roundly derided for their high amounts of cholesterol. Recently though, eggs have regained their old reputation as a good source of protein. That said, it is still a good idea to limit the amount of eggs you ingest each week. Egg substitute, available in both a refrigerated and a frozen form, is a pastuerized egg mixture with a limited amount of the cholesterol laden yolk included. Egg substitute can be used in place of eggs in nearly every dish. It is also the only egg product that should be used in dishes calling for raw eggs. Raw eggs should never be eaten due to the possibility of bacteria. Since egg substitute is pastuerized, that threat has been eliminated.

• **Enchilada Sauce**: Enchilada sauce is a sauce based on either red or green chile peppers, found in traditional Mexican dishes. It can be made at home, or is available canned in mild, medium or hot versions. Look for it in the ethnic foods section at your grocers.

• **Garbanzo beans**: Garbanzo beans are also called chick-peas or ceci beans. They are medium sized, yellow beans used in Arab and Spanish cooking, and familiar to Americans from restaurant salad bars. Garbanzos are a popular foodstuffs in Mediterranean and Middle Eastern cooking. They date back to at least 5400 B.C.E., and are an inexpensive and tasty source of protein. They can be found dried or canned with other bean products. The canned version should be drained and rinsed before use.

• **Green Chiles (canned)**: Green chiles are simply the canned version of the Verde chile, a large, mild, green pepper. Verde chiles, like all chile peppers, originated in the Americas and are often used in Mexican based dishes. Canned green chiles are available whole, chopped or diced. You will find them in the ethnic foods section of the grocers.

• **Half and Half**: Half and half is milk and light cream, combined in equal amounts. It is available in the dairy aisle, and is often used to lend a creamy texture to sauces, without adding all of the fat of heavy cream.

• **Hoisin Sauce**: Hoisin sauce is also known as Asian barbeque sauce. It is mixture of soybeans, sugar and seasonings, with a light garlic flavor and is most often used in traditional Chinese dishes. Use it as you would use any barbeque sauce. Look for it in the ethnic foods section at your grocers.

• **Pimiento (from a jar)**: Pimientos are sweet, heart shaped peppers native to the Americas, and like other peppers have a high vitamin C content. Despite being an American native, it is seldom eaten fresh in our own country, and is next to impossible to find in its fresh form. Pimiento is most commonly known to us as the red stuffing in green olives. It is usually sold canned or in a small jar, and can be found in the pickle aisle at the grocers.

• **Polenta (tube)**: Polenta, once the inexpensive diet staple of poor peasants, has recently become a star in the food world. Polenta is simply a cooked yellow corn meal mush. It can be purchased dry, like other corn meals or already cooked and packaged into a tube. Polenta is traditional Italian comfort food, but I find the tube variety a convenient substitute for any corn meal dish. Look for it with the other health food items at the grocery store.

• **Roasted red pepper**: This is another example of someone else doing the work for us. Roasted red pepper is a sweet red bell pepper that has been roasted and peeled. It is sold in a jar and is available in the canned vegetable or pickle aisle at the grocery store.

• **Soy Sauce**: Soy sauce is a condiment popular in Asian cooking. It is traditionally made from fermented soybeans, toasted wheat, barley salt and water, but there are numerous forms of soy sauce available, dark, light, thick, thin, Japanese or Chinese. Tamari, usually found in health food stores, is a more traditional form of soy sauce, and has a more complex flavor than the more commonly available soy sauces. Soy sauce can be found in the ethnic foods section of the grocers.

• **Stuffing mix**: Traditional bread stuffing brings back memories of Thanksgiving turkeys with all the trimmings. Mom would lovingly make her special stuffing, cutting up bread, adding just the right amount of herbs, and mixing it with her own secret ingredient - apples or celery or potatoes or chestnuts. Today we can dispense with hours of labor, and choose from a good assortment of dried bread cubes or crumbs, already mixed with herbs. These mixtures usually come in a bag or box, but be careful not to buy the quick-cooking kind which is high in salt. You will usually find stuffing mixtures along with instant potatoes at the grocers.

• **Sun dried tomatoes**: Drying tomatoes leads to an intense flavor, loved by some, but a little too strong for others. I fall into the first category, and put dried tomatoes on everything. Dried tomatoes are most common in the foods of the sunny Mediterranean, and you will find them in traditional Italian, Greek, and Northern African dishes. They are becoming more common here in the United States, and are available packed in oil or simply dried. Look for them in the produce aisle with the fresh tomatoes, the canned vegetable aisle, or even the spice aisle.

• **Tomato paste**: Tomato paste is the thick concentrate of cooked tomatoes. It is available in small cans - that still always seem too big to me. If you are fortunate, you can find tomato paste in a squeeze tube, a much more convenient package. Like all highly concentrated foods, tomato paste has an intense flavor, and a little goes a long way. Make sure to put leftovers in your freezer "tomato" container to make sauce at a later date. You will find tomato paste with other canned tomato products at the grocery store.

• **Tortillas**: Tortillas are an unleavened bread, traditional to Mexico, but related to other unleavened breads of the Middle East and India. Tortillas are made of corn or flour and can be rolled or folded and filled with numerous ingredients. Flour tortillas are great to keep on hand for a quick snack. My children used to fill a tortilla with a slice of cheese and asparagus spears and pop it in the microwave for nutritious and filling snack. Look for tortillas in either the bread aisle or the ethnic foods section at your grocers.

• **Vermicelli**: Vermicelli, which actually means "little worms" is a very thin spaghetti-like pasta. Other thin pastas, spaghetti, linguini or angel hair can be used in place of vermicelli. Look for it with the dried pastas and noodles at the grocery store.

ENTREE TERMS

• **Jambalaya:** Jambalaya is spicy Cajun or Creole rice dish, commonly available in southern Louisiana. Jambalayas may include a variety of ham, sausage, shellfish, beans and vegetables, and traditionally include that southern favorite, okra.

• **Panini**: Panini are Italian rolls. However, the term is most often used in the United States to identify a lightly grilled, pressed sandwich.

• **Quiche**: Quiche is basically a savory, as opposed to sweet, custard baked in a pie shell. The most famous quiche, quiche Lorraine, hales from the Lorraine region of France and is a rich custard with cheese and bacon. Quiches are a simple way to add a fancy touch to any meal.

• **Ragoût**: Ragoût is the French term for a thick, highly seasoned stew.

• **Ratatouille**: Yet another delicious favorite we borrow from the French. Ratatouille is a versatile mixture of zucchini, tomatoes, bell peppers, eggplant and seasonings and can be served either hot or cold. It is especially tasty in the late summer, when all of the ingredients are garden fresh.

BASIC RECIPES

As you read through the recipes in this book, you will notice that some called for items that are already prepared to some degree. Many of these you can purchase at the local store, but some you may want to fix yourself. This section of basic recipes shows you how to do just that. Some are easy - if you can boil water you can hard boil an egg for example - others show you how to re-create some old fashioned favorites like homemade pie crust and creamy polenta. You will find everything you need here to complete a fast, easy, delicious meal. Enjoy.

Bacon: *Bacon can be cooked by pan-frying, broiling, or in the microwave.*

Pan-fry:Place bacon in an unheated skillet. Cook over medium-low heat for 6-8 minutes. Turn the bacon often while cooking. Drain.

Broil:Place bacon slices on the broiler pan. Broil 3-5 inches from the heat source until the bacon is done. Turn once while broiling. Watch the bacon closely while broiling to avoid burning.

Microwave:Place bacon on a microwave safe plate. Cook on high heat level for 2-10 minutes, in 2 minute increments, depending on the number of bacon slices you are cooking at one time.

Bread Crumbs:*Making your own bread crumbs is a great way to use stale bread. Crumbs can be soft or dried, plain or mixed with herbs. All recipes in this book that call for bread crumbs use dried crumbs.*

Soft crumbs: The simplest way to make soft crumbs is to cut the bread into cubes and place in a food processor or blender for 10 - 20 seconds.

Soft crumbs can also be made by rubbing slices of bread against a hand held grater.

Dried crumbs:Spread soft bread crumbs on a baking sheet. Bake at 275°F until lightly toasted, 5-10 minutes. Watch closely so they don't burn, and stir at least once while cooking.

Cellophane Noodles:*Cellophane noodles are the easiest of all pastas to cook.*

Place noodles in a heat safe bowl. Cover the noodles with boiling water. Cover the bowl with a plate, and allow the noodles to sit for 5 minutes. Drain and rinse.

Chicken:*Cooked chicken can be purchased at the grocery store in a variety of ways; packaged with the sandwich meats,* *sliced from the deli, or whole from the deli. Sometimes though, you may want to save money and cook your own. Cooking chicken is very simple and the result can be refrigerated for 2-3 days, or frozen for up to a month.*

1. Use either a whole chicken or chicken parts. Chicken breasts will provide you with white meat, chicken legs and thighs with dark meat. Wash the chicken and place in a large pot.
2. Cover the chicken with water. Bring to a boil, and then cook over medium heat until the chicken is cooked through (no pink meat). Check to assure that the chicken is done by pulling a thick piece of the meat apart with a fork.
3. Drain and cool.
4. Remove the skin and cut the chicken meat into pieces.
5. Use as directed in each individual recipe.

Corn on the Cob: *For some of us, fresh corn on the cob is like ambrosia, food fit for the gods. There are many ways to cook corn on the cob, all of them good. But simply boiling the ears is the easiest and quickest way I know.*

Fresh corn ears

1. Husk the ears of corn and remove the corn silk.
2. Place the ears in a large pot, and cover with water.
3. Bring the water to a boil. Reduce heat slightly and boil corn for 6-8 minutes.
4. Remove ears from pot and serve immediately with butter, salt, and pepper.

Cous Cous: *Cous cous is actually tiny grains of pasta. It is a very popular dish in Northern Africa and the Middle East. Its cooking method nearly the same as that for cellophane noodles.*

> 1. Place cous cous in a heat safe bowl or pot.
> 2 .Add boiling water or broth, 1 ¼ cup for each cup of cous cous.
> 3. Stir and cover. Let sit for 15 minutes while the cous cous steams.
> 4. Fluff the cooked cous cous with a fork before serving.

Eggs: *For many of us, hard boiled eggs are the first thing we learn to cook. And a useful skill it is. A hard boiled egg can be sliced and added to salads, mashed and made into egg salad, cut in half and deviled, placed in vinegar and pickled, or eaten as is with a little salt.*

> 1. Place eggs in a pot, large enough so that they are not layered on each other. Cover with cold water.
> 2. Bring to a full boil over medium-high heat. Reduce heat to medium, but still boiling.
> 3. Cook for 10 minutes. If you are not sure if your eggs are done at this point, cut one of them in half. If the yolk is still runny, cook for an additional two minutes.
> 4. Drain and rinse with cold water. Peel and enjoy.

Herbs: *Growing and drying your own herbs is easy and tasty. Herbs can be grown in pots on your windowsill, or outside* *during the summer.*

Wait until herbs are just starting to flower. Cut close to their base. Tie together and hang upside down until herbs have dried, usually 1 - 4 days. Rub dried leaves off of stems and store in a cool place.

Pie Crust:*Making really good pie crust requires patience and practice. Although you can buy refrigerated or frozen pie crusts just about anywhere now, the homemade version is much better. That said, it does take time to make you own pie crust - but the results are worth it. The key to a good pie crust is to use very cold water.*

> 1 ½ cups of flour
> ½ tsp. salt
> ½ cup shortening
> 4 to 5 Tbsp. cold water

1. In a large bowl, mix flour and salt.
2. Cut in shortening until pieces are the size of small peas.
3. Sprinkle water over the mixture, one tablespoon at a time. Carefully mix with a fork. Do not over mix.
4. Form dough into a ball.
5. Roll out dough on a lightly floured surface. Fit pastry into pie plate.
6. Fold under and flute the edges. Bake at 450°F for 10 to 12 minutes, or as directed in each recipe. Makes one pie crust.

Polenta: *Homemade polenta makes a soft, mushy dish - good served as is or it can be refrigerated and then sliced. Use a large pan to cook the polenta, as it has a tendency to bubble and spit as it cooks!*

1 cup coarse-grained, yellow cornmeal
1 tsp. salt
4 ½ cups water

1. In a large pot, bring the water to a boil.
2. Reduce heat to medium-high. Add salt. Stir.
3. Add the cornmeal, ¼ cup at a time. Stir after each addition.
4. Continue stirring continuously for 30 - 45 minutes, being careful to keep the cornmeal mixture from burning. Reduce heat to medium if desired. When it is done, the polenta should be thick and shiny. Serve immediately with sauce, or refrigerate for later. Serves 2.

Potato: *For some people, there is nothing like a baked potato. I'm not much of a potato fan myself, but there are times when a baked potato rounds out the meal perfectly. Light and fluffy russet potatoes are the best to bake (they are the long, brown ones), but this method works just as well with sweet potatoes too.*

Raw potatoes

1. Preheat oven to 425°F. Wash potatoes and pierce once or twice with a fork.

2. Place potatoes in the oven directly on the oven rack. Bake for 40 - 60 minutes. Check to see if potatoes are done by pushing a fork into them. If the potato is not completely cooked, you will feel some resistance.

3. Remove potatoes from the oven. Cut across the top and push in the ends to open the potato up. Serve with butter or sour cream.

Rice: *When I was a child we never had rice, probably for a variety of reasons, but also because my mother thought it was difficult to cook properly. Today's inexpensive rice cookers make cooking rice very easy. But even if you don't own a rice cooker, you can easily make rice from scratch. The key is not to use a high temperature setting.*

1 cup long, medium or short grain rice
2 ¼ cups water
Dash salt

1. Mix the rice, water, and salt in a large pot. Bring to a boil.

2. Stir. Reduce heat to medium-low and cover the pot.

3.Let rice mixture steam for 15 minutes. If the water continues to bubble over the sides of the pot, reduce heat further. Do not lift cover while rice is cooking.

4. Remove rice from heat. All of the water should be absorbed by the rice. If not, continue to cook for 5 minutes more. Stir with a fork to fluff. Let the rice sit for 5 minutes before serving.

Roasted Red Pepper: *Peppers are very easy to roast, and have a more robust flavor than the canned variety. However, sometimes it is more economical to buy the already prepared version. If you have a few extra red peppers though, try this easy method.*

Peppers
Vegetable oil

1. Preheat the oven to 425°F.
2. Wash and dry the whole peppers. Brush the outside lightly with the oil.
3. Place on a pan and place the pan in the upper part of the oven. Turn the peppers every 5 - 7 minutes. Continue cooking for 20 -25 minutes, or until the skin of the peppers starts to blister.
4. Remove from oven and let cool.
5. Core and peel the peppers. They are now ready to use.

Sauce (thickened broth): *The microwave is the very easiest way to make a thickened broth sauce. However, it's always nice to know how to do it the old fashioned way too. The key is not to cook the broth too fast or too hot.*

2 Tbsp. butter or margarine
2 Tbsp. flour
Dash salt
1 cup chicken, beef or vegetable broth

1. Melt the butter in a saucepan over medium heat.
2. Add the flour and salt and stir to mix well.

3. Add the broth all at once. Cook, stirring constantly until the broth thickens and bubbles.

4. Remove from heat and add to the appropriate recipe. Makes one cup of sauce.

Note: Chopped celery, onion, carrots, or other vegetables may be added at step one. Lightly cook the vegetables until they are crisp tender, and then continue on with step two.

Sauce (Cream sauce):*Again, the microwave is the easiest way to make a cream or cheese sauce. You may find it difficult to get your cream sauce to thicken in the microwave when the weather is humid however. It does work better on the stove top during those sultry days.*

2 Tbsp. butter or margarine
2 Tbsp. flour
Dash salt
1 cup milk

1. Melt the butter in a medium saucepan over medium heat.

2. Add the flour and salt and stir to mix well.

3. Add the milk all at once. Cook, stirring constantly until milk thickens and bubbles.

4. Remove from heat and add to the appropriate recipe. Makes one cup of sauce.

Note: To make a cheese sauce, add $1/3$ cup of shredded cheese after removing the thickened sauce from the heat source. Stir until the cheese melts.

Taco Seasoning Mix: *I have this very bad habit of running out of taco seasoning mix at the most inopportune times. Out of necessity I have started making my own. This mix will have a little more zing than the commercial variety, and a lot less salt. You may want to use a little bit less than the recipe calls for in the beginning, and adjust to fit your own taste.*

2 tsp. instant minced onion
2 tsp. chili powder
1 tsp. ground cumin
1 tsp. salt
½ tsp. crushed red pepper
½ tsp. instant minced garlic
¼ tsp. dried oregano leaves
1 tsp. flour or cornstarch

1. Mix all ingredients together.
2. Makes approximately ¼ cup of taco seasoning mix.

THE WELL STOCKED PANTRY

Keeping your pantry well stocked will save you time, energy, and angst when it comes to fixing dinner. The recipes included in *"I Want My Dinner Now!"* are based on having some specific items in the cupboard at all times. Try to keep as many of these basic pantry items on hand as possible.

HERBS AND SPICES

Basil: Dried leaves
Bay Leaf
Cajun Seasoning mix
Chili Powder
Cinnamon
Curry Powder
Garlic: Instant, minced

Ginger: Ground
Lemon-Pepper Seasoning
Marjoram: Dried leaves

Mustard: Dry
Onion: Instant, minced
Oregano: Dried leaves
Paprika
Pepper: Black
Pepper: Crushed red
Pepper: Ground red
        (Cayenne)
Rosemary: Dried
Salt
Thyme: Dried
Turmeric

CANNED GOODS

Beans: Garbanzo
Beans: Kidney
Soup: Low fat Cream of Celery

Tomatoes: Diced
Tomato: Paste
Tomato: Sauce

DRIED GOODS

Noodles: Egg
Pasta (spaghetti or other thin pasta, elbows, ziti or other tube
        pasta, orzo or other small)
Rice: White
Rice: Brown
Rice: Quick cooking brown

CONDIMENTS AND OTHER FIXINGS

Broth or Bouillon: Beef
Broth or Bouillon: Chicken
Broth or Bouillon: Vegetable
Bread Crumbs
Butter or Margarine
Eggs
Honey
Ketchup
Lemon juice
Mayonnaise

Milk
Molasses
Mustard: Prepared
Peanut Butter
Pepper Sauce: Hot
Soy Sauce
Vegetable Oil
Vinegar: Cider
Vinegar: Red Wine

BAKING GOODS

Baking Powder
Brown Sugar
Cornstarch
Flour
White Sugar

FAST AND SIMPLE

It was one of those days at work. Yet another "it feels like Monday" day. You got home late. Your son will be home soon from soccer practice but your daughter's band recital is tonight. Or maybe you are cooking for yourself, but have a big exam tomorrow and don't relish the thought of spending hours over the stove - and even more time cleaning up afterwards. Either way, you need something *Fast and Simple* for dinner. Something easy to prepare, that doesn't use many ingredients, and that both you and the kids will eat. Something that won't take a huge bite out of your grocery budget. Luckily, you have come to the right place. The recipes in this section:

* Can be on the table in 35 minutes or less.

* Use common, everyday ingredients.

* Use easy-to-store products. No garlic cloves to peel, no onions to chop.

* Are designed for today's tastes. These are the same entrees you order in a restaurant, without all the salt and fat.

* Have easy-to-follow directions with few steps.

* Provide hearty servings that even satisfy growing boys.

* Don't leave you with many dirty dishes to wash.

* Provide a little something for everyone; meats, chicken, vegetables, meatless.

Fast and Simple

Time: 25 minutes

PIZZA BURGERS

Top these tangy burgers with sliced onion, tomato and mozzarella cheese.

2 Servings	Ingredients	6 Servings
½ lb.	Ground beef	1 ½ lb.
1	Egg	1
2 Tbsp	Parmesan cheese	6 Tbsp
1 tsp	Instant minced onion	1 Tbsp
½ tsp	Instant minced garlic	1 tsp
½ tsp	Dried basil leaves	1 tsp
½ tsp	Dried oregano leaves	1 tsp
¼ tsp	Crushed red pepper	½ tsp
¼ cup	Bread crumbs	¾ cup
1 Tbsp	Pizza sauce	3 Tbsp

1. In a large bowl, combine all ingredients. Mix well.
2. Shape mixture into patties, one for each serving.
3. Grill over medium-hot coals and cook as desired, about 10 minutes for medium, 15 minutes for medium-well. Turn once while grilling.
Or
3. Place burgers on broiler pan. Broil 4 inches from heat until cooked as desired, about 10 minutes for medium, 15 minutes for medium-well. Turn once while broiling.

Pantry Items:
Eggs, seasonings, bread crumbs

Grocery Items:
Ground beef, Parmesan cheese, pizza sauce

Serve With:

 Hamburger buns and pasta salad.

Time: 25 minutes

TACO SALAD

Top this quick salad with sour cream and your favorite salsa.

2 Servings	Ingredients	6 Servings
1/3 lb.	Ground beef	1 lb
2/3 cup	Canned kidney beans	2 cups
½ cup	Lettuce	1 ½ cups
1	Tomatoes	3
1 ½ Tbsp	Taco seasoning mix	¼ cup
¼ cup	Water	¾ cup
¼ tsp.	Chili powder	¾ tsp
2 cups	Nacho chips	6 cups
¼ cup	Shredded cheese	¾ cup
6 inch	Skillet	12 inch

1. Brown ground beef in skillet over medium heat, 5-10 minutes. Drain and rinse kidney beans, set aside. Chop tomatoes and lettuce, set aside.
2. Add taco seasoning mix, chili powder, beans, and water to ground beef in the skillet..
3. Bring to boil. Reduce heat and simmer for 10 minutes.
4. Break chips into bite sized pieces. Put 1 cup of chips in each serving plate. Top with hot ground beef mixture. Top with cheese, lettuce and tomatoes.

 Serve With:

Cornbread

Pantry Items:
Kidney beans, chili powder

Grocery Items:
Ground beef, taco seasoning, chips, lettuce, tomato, cheese

Time: 35 minutes

BARBEQUE MEATBALLS

This dish has been a family favorite for generations. It is equally good stuffed into a hoagy roll, or served over hot cooked noodles.

2 Servings	Ingredients	6 Servings
½ lb	Ground beef	1 ½ lb
1 ½ tsp	Instant minced onion	1 ½ Tbsp
1	Egg	1
2 Tbsp	Bread crumbs	6 Tbsp
1 ½ tsp	Vegetable oil	1 ½ Tbsp
1 cup	Tomato sauce	3 cups
2 Tbsp	Brown sugar	6 Tbsp
1 Tbsp	Vinegar	3 Tbsp
1 tsp	Prepared mustard	1 Tbsp
6 inch	Skillet	12 inch

1. In a bowl, combine ground beef, onion, egg, and bread crumbs.
2. Shape mixture into small balls.
3. Heat oil in skillet over medium heat. Brown meatballs, 5-10 minutes.
4. Combine tomato sauce, sugar, vinegar and mustard. Pour over meatballs.
5. Cover and cook over medium-low heat for 15 minutes, or until meatballs are cooked through.

Pantry Items:
Dried onion, egg, oil, bread crumbs , tomato sauce, brown sugar, vinegar, mustard

Grocery Items:
Ground beef

 Serve With:
A green salad or steamed broccoli.

Time: 20 minutes

BEEF STIR-FRY

2 Servings	Ingredients	6 Servings
½ lb	Flank steak	1 ½ lb.
⅓ cup	Bell Pepper	1 cup
1 Tbsp	Vegetable oil	3 Tbsp
1 ½ cup	Frozen broccoli, cauliflower mix	4 ½ cups
¼ cup	Beef broth	¾ cup
2 Tbsp	Red wine vinegar	6 Tbsp
1 ½ tsp	Instant minced onion	1 ½ Tbsp
1 ½ tsp	Cornstarch	1 ½ Tbsp
6 inch	Skillet or Wok	12 inch

1. Cut steak into thin strips. Chop bell pepper.
2. Heat oil in skillet over medium-high heat.
3. Stir-fry steak and bell pepper in oil until steak is no longer red and pepper is crisp-tender, 4 -5 minutes.
4. Add frozen vegetables to skillet. Cover and cook over medium-low heat until cooked through, about 10 minutes.
5. Meanwhile, broth, vinegar, onion and cornstarch and let sit while meat and vegetables are cooking. The liquid will re-hydrate the dried onion.
6. Add liquid mixture to skillet. Cook and stir until bubbly, 2-3 minutes.

Serve With: Cooked pasta or rice. Top with grated Parmesan cheese.

Cook's Tip: The beef will be easier to slice if partially frozen

Pantry Items:
Oil, broth, vinegar, dried onion, cornstarch

Grocery Items:
Flank steak, bell pepper, frozen vegetables

Time: 20 -35 minutes

MOM'S HAM STEAK

When I was a child, Sunday dinner often included Mom's glazed ham. Here, I keep the same flavor using an easier-to-cook ham steak.

2 Servings	Ingredients	6 Servings
½ lb	Ham slice, ½ " thick	1 ½ lb
¼ cup	Ginger Ale	¾ cup
1 (8oz. can)	Canned pineapple chunks	1 (16 oz.can)
1 Tbsp	Brown sugar	3 Tbsp
1 tsp	Prepared mustard	1 Tbsp
6 inch	Skillet	10 inch

1. Place ham slice in skillet. Add ginger ale and pineapple, undrained.
2. Cover and cook over medium heat until nearly done; 10-15 minutes for pre-cooked ham, 20 -25 minutes for bone-in ham.
3. Combine brown sugar and mustard. Spread on ham. Return cover and cook for 5 more minutes.

Pantry Items:
Brown sugar, mustard

Grocery Items:
Ham slice, ginger ale, canned pineapple

 Serve With:
Mixed vegetables and baked sweet potato

Time: 30 minutes

APPLE SAUCED PORK CHOPS

Pork and fruit just naturally go together.

2 Servings	Ingredients	6 Servings
2	Pork chops	6
1 small	Sweet potato	2 medium
1 small	Apples	2 medium
1 tsp	Vegetable oil	1 Tbsp
½ cup	Apple juice	1 ½ cups
¼ tsp	Cinnamon	¾ tsp
1 tsp	Cornstarch	1 Tbsp
8 inch	Skillet	12 inch

1. Trim fat from pork chops. Peel sweet potato and slice into ¼ inch rounds. Peel and core apples and cut into thin wedges.
2. Heat oil in skillet over medium heat. Brown chops, turning once - about 5 minutes.
3. Add sliced sweet potato and apple juice to skillet. Cover and simmer for 10 minutes. Add apple slices to skillet.
4. Continue cooking for an additional 5 - 10 minutes or until chops are cooked through and sweet potato is soft.
5. Combine cinnamon, cornstarch and ½ cup water. Stir into skillet.
6. Cook, stirring constantly until sauce is slightly thickened and bubbly, 2-3 minutes.

Pantry Items:
Oil, cinnamon, cornstarch

Grocery Items:
Pork chops, apple juice, sweet potato, apples

Serve With:

 Steamed broccoli or green beans, and cranberry sauce.

Time: 25 minutes

ZITI WITH BACON

Adding a few drops of hot sauce will enhance the cheese flavor and give this dish extra zing.

2 Servings	Ingredients	6 Servings
3 oz. (1 cup)	Ziti or other tubular pasta	9 oz. (3 cups)
$\frac{1}{3}$ cup	Bell Pepper	1 cup
2 small (2 cups)	Zucchini	6 small (6 cups)
2 slices	Bacon	6 slices
1 ½ tsp	Flour	1 ½ Tbsp
dash	Black pepper	¼ tsp
$\frac{2}{3}$ cup	Milk	2 cups
¼ cup	Parmesan cheese	¾ cup
6 inch	Skillet	12 inch

1. Cook ziti according to package directions. Drain.
2. While ziti is cooking, dice bacon strips, chop bell pepper and slice zucchini.
3. Cook bacon in skillet over medium heat. Discard all but one Tablespoon of bacon drippings.
4. Add bell pepper and zucchini to skillet. Stir-fry until vegetables are crisp tender.
5. Mix flour, pepper and milk. Stir into mixture in skillet. Cook, stirring constantly until sauce is slightly thickened.
6. Pour thickened sauce over drained pasta in pot. Add the Parmesan cheese and toss gently.

Pantry Items:
Pasta, flour, milk, pepper

Grocery Items:
Bell pepper, bacon, zucchini, Parmesan cheese

 Serve With:
Simple green salad of lettuce and tomato

53

Time: 20 minutes

CREAMY CHICKEN AND MUSHROOMS

Using skinless, boneless chicken breasts or tenders will save you time.

2 Servings	Ingredients	6 Servings
2	Chicken breasts	6
1 Tbsp	Vegetable oil	3 Tbsp
¼ cup	Canned mushrooms, drained	¾ cup
1 cup	Frozen broccoli	3 cups
2 Tbsp	Flour	6 Tbsp
1 cup	Chicken broth	3 cups
1 tsp	Instant minced onion	1 Tbsp
½ tsp	Instant minced garlic	1 tsp
dash	Black pepper	¼ tsp
1 cup	Sour cream	3 cups
6 inch	Skillet	12 inch

1. Cut chicken into bite-sized pieces.
2. Heat oil in skillet over medium heat. Stir-fry chicken until no longer pink, about 5 minutes.
3. Add drained mushrooms and broccoli. Reduce heat to medium-low. Cover and cook until heated through, about 5 minutes.
4. In a small bowl, combine flour, broth, onion, garlic and pepper Add to skillet. Cook and stir gently till bubbly, 2-3 minutes.
5. Gently fold in sour cream. Serve immediately.

 Serve With: Serve over cooked green noodles or biscuits.

Pantry Items:
Oil, flour, seasonings, broth

Grocery Items:
Chicken breasts, mushrooms, broccoli, sour cream

Time: 35 minutes

SKILLET CHICKEN PAELLA

Paella is a Spanish rice dish, with roots in Northern African cusine.

2 Servings	Ingredients	6 Servings
1	Skinless, boneless chicken breasts	3
1 Tbsp	Vegetable oil	3 Tbsp
½ cup	Bell Pepper, chopped	1 cup
1 tsp	Instant minced onion	1 Tbsp
½ tsp	Instant minced garlic	1 tsp
½ tsp	Dried oregano leaves	1 tsp
1 cup	Chicken broth	3 cups
$\frac{1}{3}$ cup	Uncooked rice	1 cup
¼ tsp	Paprika	¾ tsp
dash	Black pepper	¼ tsp
¼ tsp	Turmeric	½ tsp
½ cup	Canned, stewed tomatoes	1 can (2 cups)
½ cup	Frozen peas	1 ½ cups
8 inch	Covered skillet	12 inch

1. Cut chicken into bite-sized pieces.

2. Heat cooking oil in skillet over medium heat. Add chicken and stir fry 3-4 minutes.

3. Add bell pepper and continue stir frying until chicken is no longer pink, 3-4 more minutes.

Pantry Items:
Oil, seasonings, rice, broth

Grocery Items:
Stewed tomatoes, bell pepper

4. Add onion, garlic, oregano, broth, rice, paprika, pepper and turmeric to skillet and stir. Bring to boil. Reduce heat, cover and simmer for 15 minutes.

5. Add undrained tomatoes and peas. Cover and simmer for 5 more minutes, or until liquid is absorbed.

 Serve With:
Green salad and crusty bread or rolls.

Time: 30 minutes

HERBED CHICKEN STIR FRY

Use skinless, boneless chicken breasts to make preparation a snap!

2 Servings	Ingredients	6 Servings
1 Tbsp	Flour	3 Tbsp
1 tsp	Instant minced onion	1 Tbsp
½ tsp	Instant minced garlic	1 ½ tsp
½ tsp	Paprika	1 tsp
½ tsp	Dried basil leaves	1 tsp
¾ cup	Chicken broth	2 ¼ cup
2 small (2 cups)	Zucchini	4 small (4 cups)
1 large	Tomatoes	3 large
⅓ cup	Bell Pepper	1 cup
1	Chicken breasts	3
1 Tbsp	Vegetable oil	3 Tbsp
6 inch	Skillet	12 inch

1. Combine flour, onion, garlic, paprika, basil and broth. Mix well. Set aside.

2. Slice zucchini into rounds and cut tomatoes into wedges. Chop bell pepper. Cut chicken into one inch pieces.

3. Add oil to skillet. Stir-fry bell pepper over medium heat until crisp-tender, 3-4 minutes.

4. Remove bell pepper from skillet. Add chicken. Stir-fry until no longer pink, about 5 minutes. Remove from skillet.

5. Add more oil to skillet if necessary. Add zucchini and stir-fry 3-4 minutes.

6. Return bell pepper and chicken to skillet. Add tomatoes and mixture from step 1. Stir gently until mixture thickens and is warmed through, 2-3 minutes.

Pantry Items:
Flour, seasonings, oil, broth

Grocery Items:
Bell pepper, chicken, zucchini, tomatoes,

 Serve With:
Serve over cooked noodles or rice.

Time: 25 minutes

SWEET AND SOUR CHICKEN

This Chinese favorite can easily be made at home, with less fat and more flavor than the restaurant version.

2 Servings	Ingredients	6 Servings
2	Boneless chicken breasts	6
⅓ cup	Bell Pepper	1 cup
2 (½ cup)	Carrots	6 (1 ½ cups)
1 Tbsp	Vegetable oil	3 Tbsp
1 (8oz. can)	Can chunk pineapple	3 (8oz cans)
2 Tbsp	Vinegar	6 Tbsp
3 Tbsp	Brown sugar	½ cup
½ tsp	Ground ginger	1 ½ tsp
2 Tbsp	Soy sauce	6 Tbsp
1 Tbsp	Cornstarch	3 Tbsp
6 inch	Skillet	12 inch

1. Cut chicken into 1 inch pieces. Slice bell pepper and carrots.
2. Heat oil in skillet over medium-high heat. Stir-fry chicken until browned, about 5 minutes.
3. Add carrots and bell pepper. Cover, reduce heat to medium-low. Simmer for 10 minutes or until vegetables are crisp-tender.

4. Combine canned pineapple (do not drain), vinegar, brown sugar, ginger, soy sauce and cornstarch. Add to skillet and stir gently over medium heat until mixture thickens slightly.

Pantry Items:
Oil, brown sugar, ginger soy sauce, cornstarch

Grocery Items:
Chicken, bell pepper, carrots, pineapple

 Serve With:
Serve with rice and purchased egg rolls or pot stickers.

Time: 15 minutes

FRUITY CHICKEN SALAD

A great way to use up leftover chicken or turkey. No leftovers? Buy pre-cooked chicken in the prepared meat aisle.

2 Servings	Ingredients	6 Servings
½ cup	Seedless grapes	1 ½ cups
1 stalk (⅓ cup)	Celery	3 stalks (1 cup)
½ cup	Apple	1 cup
1 cup	Cooked chicken	3 cups
¼ cup	Mayonnaise	¾ cup
1 tsp	Lemon juice	1 Tbsp

1. Slice the grapes and chop the apple and celery. Chop the chicken.
2. In a bowl, add all ingredients and mix well.
3. Add salt and pepper to taste.

 Serve With:

Scoop onto lettuce leaves or stuff a pita or hamburger bun.
Add a bowl tomato soup for a light but satisfying supper.

Pantry Items:

Mayonnaise, lemon juice

 Cook's Tip:

Use low-fat yogurt instead of mayonnaise to add a tangy flavor and reduce fat.

Grocery Items:
Chicken, celery, grapes, apple

Time: 35 minutes

CHICKEN CACCIATORE

Both boneless and bone-in chicken breasts work well in this Italian favorite.

2 Servings	Ingredients	6 Servings
1 Tbsp	Vegetable oil	3 Tbsp
2	Chicken breasts	6
1 cup.	Canned tomatoes, diced	3 cups
½ cup	Tomato puree	1 (12 oz.can)
2 Tbsp	Chicken broth	$^1/_3$ cup
$^1/_3$ cup	Bell Pepper, chopped	1 cup
1 tsp	Instant minced onion	1 Tbsp
½ tsp	Instant minced garlic	1 tsp
½ tsp	Dried basil leaves	1 tsp
½ tsp	Dried oregano leaves	1 tsp
6 inch	Skillet	12 inch

1. Heat oil in skillet over medium heat. Remove skin and discard if not using skinless chicken.
2. Add chicken breasts and brown, 3-4 minutes.
3. Add remaining ingredients. Bring to boil. Cover skillet and reduce heat to medium-low. Simmer for 30 minutes, or until chicken is tender.

Pantry Items:
Oil, seasonings, canned tomatoes, broth

Grocery Items:
Chicken Breasts, tomato puree, bell pepper

 Serve With: Cooked rice, noodles, or baked potato. Add a green vegetable to portray the colors of the Italian flag, red, green and white!

 Cook's Tip:
A cut up, fryer chicken may be used instead of chicken breasts if you prefer.

Time: 30 minutes

CHICKEN CURRY

The curry powder commonly available in the United States is usually sweet, not hot. If you prefer a hot curry, use a small amount of curry paste in place of the powder.

2 Servings	Ingredients	6 Servings
1 tsp	Curry powder	1 Tbsp
1 tsp	Paprika	1 Tbsp
1 tsp	Ground ginger	2 ½ tsp
dash	Black pepper	¼ tsp
1 small	Sweet potato	2 medium
2	Boneless chicken breasts or tenders	6
1 Tbsp	Vegetable oil	3 Tbsp
½ cup	Coconut milk	1 (14oz can)
¼ cup	Chicken broth	¾cup
6 inch	Skillet	12 inch

1. Combine curry powder, paprika, ginger and pepper. Set aside.
2. Peel and dice sweet potato.
3. Cut chicken into 1 inch pieces. Toss chicken with the seasoning mix from step 1.
4. Heat oil in skillet over medium-high heat.
5. Stir-fry chicken until no longer pink, about 5 minutes.
6. Add sweet potato, coconut milk, and chicken broth to skillet.
7. Cover and continue cooking over medium heat, stirring often, until sweet potato and chicken are cooked through, 10-15 minutes.

Pantry Items:
Seasonings, oil, broth

Grocery Items:
Chicken, sweet potato, coconut milk

 Serve with:

Spinach and mushroom salad, steamed rice and chutney.

Time: 30 minutes

ORANGE CHICKEN STIR-FRY

Serve over cooked rice, noodles, or angel hair pasta.

2 Servings	Ingredients	6 Servings
2	Boneless chicken breasts or tenders	6
1 ½ Tbsp	Vegetable oil	3 Tbsp
1 ½ cups	Frozen broccoli, cauliflower, carrot mix	1 (16 oz bag)
2 Tbsp	Orange juice	6 Tbsp
1 ½ tsp	Soy sauce	1 ½ Tbsp
1 Tbsp	Honey	3 Tbsp
½ cup	Chicken broth	1 ½ cup
½ tsp	Ground ginger	1 ½ tsp
1 Tbsp	Cornstarch	3 Tbsp
6 inc	Skillet	12 inch

1. Cut chicken into 1 inch pieces.
2. Heat oil in skillet over medium heat. Stir fry chicken until lightly browned, 5-10 minutes.
3. Reduce heat to medium-low. Add vegetables. Cover and simmer until warmed through, about 10 minutes.

4. In a small bowl, combine orange juice, soy sauce, honey, broth, ginger and cornstarch. Pour into skillet. Stir gently over medium heat until heated through and sauce thickens slightly, 2-3 minutes.

Pantry Items:
Oil, soy sauce, honey, cornstarch, broth

Grocery Items:
Chicken breasts, frozen vegetables, orange juice

 Serve With: A green or fruit salad.

Time: 25 minutes

CHICKEN AND DUMPLINGS

Don't be put off by the long ingredient list. This meal goes together quickly and tastes just as good as Mom's.

2 Servings	Ingredients	6 Servings
1 ½ cups	Chicken broth	4 ½ cups
1 ½ cups	Frozen vegetable mix	4 ½ cups
1 ½ tsp	Instant minced onion	1 ½ Tbsp
1 tsp	Instant minced garlic	1 Tbsp
½ tsp	Dried basil leaves	1 tsp
dash	Black pepper	¼ tsp
1 cup	Cooked chicken, chopped	3 cups
⅓ cup	Flour	1 cup
1 tsp	Baking powder	3 tsp
2 Tbsp	Milk	⅓ cup
1 Tbsp	Vegetable oil	1 Tbsp
2 tsp	Cornstarch	2 tsp
¼ cup	Water	¼ cup
⅓ cup	Sour cream	1 cup

10 inch	Saucepan	Dutch Oven

1. Combine broth, vegetables, onion, garlic, basil, pepper and chicken in saucepan. Heat to boiling, reduce heat to medium-low.

2. Meanwhile, in a small bowl combine flour, baking powder, milk, oil.

3. Drop flour mixture by the spoonful onto hot chicken-vegetable mixture.

4. Cover and let dumplings steam, about 15 minutes. Do not lift cover.

5. Remove dumplings. Mix the cornstarch and ¼ cup water. Stir into chicken mixture. Mixture should thicken almost immediately.

6. Gently stir in sour cream. Serve with dumplings.

Pantry Items:
Seasonings, flour, baking powder, oil, broth

Grocery Items:
Frozen vegetables, chicken, sour cream

 **Serve With:**
Cooked noodles and green beans

Time: 35 minutes

VEGETABLE CURRY

Bring home the exotic flavors of Indian fare with this simple-to-prepare curry.

2 Servings	Ingredients	6 Servings
1 cup (about 6)	Small red potatoes	3 cups (about 18)
1 cup	Fresh or frozen cauliflower	3 cups
¼ cup	Bell Pepper,	¾ cup
$1/_3$ cup	Canned garbanzo beans	1 cup
1 cup	Vegetable broth	3 cups
½ tsp	Instant minced onion	1 ½ tsp
¼ tsp	Ground ginger	½ tsp
¼ tsp	Instant minced garlic	½ tsp
½ tsp	Curry powder	1 tsp
¼ cup	Frozen peas	½ cup
½ cup	Sour cream	1 ½ cup

2 quart	Saucepan	Dutch Oven

1. Cut potatoes into quarters. Do not peel. If using fresh cauliflower, cut into small florets. Chop bell pepper and drain garbanzo beans.

3. Add potatoes, cauliflower, bell pepper, beans, broth, onion, ginger, garlic, curry powder and peas to saucepan. Mix well.

4. Bring to boil. Cover and reduce heat to medium until all vegetables are cooked through, about 20 minutes.

5. Remove from heat. Gently stir in sour cream.

Pantry Items: Broth, dried onion, ground ginger, dried garlic, curry powder, garbanzo beans.

Grocery Items: Bell pepper, potatoes, cauliflower, peas, sour cream

 Serve With: Steamed rice or cous cous and flat bread.

☺ **Cook's Tip:** If you prefer a hot curry, substitute curry paste for the curry powder.

Time: 20 minutes

GREEK FRITTATA

My husband is an expert at making omelets, but I lack this skill. My omelets always look as if they had been dropped on the floor. Luckily, frittatas are easier to make, and look and taste just as good as omelets.

2 Servings	Ingredients	6 Servings
1 small (1 cup)	Zucchini	3 small (3 cups)
1 Tbsp	Vegetable oil	3 Tbsp
1 ½ tsp	Instant minced onion	1 ½ Tbsp
½ tsp	Dried basil leaves	1 tsp
dash	Salt	¼ tsp
¼ tsp	Black pepper	½ tsp
2 Tbsp	Milk	6 Tbsp
3	Large eggs	9
2 ounces	Feta cheese, crumbled	6 ounces
6 inch	Skillet	12 inch

1. Cut zucchini lengthwise into 4 quarters and slice thinly.
2. Heat oil in skillet over medium heat. Add zucchini and saute until tender, 3-4 minutes.
3. In a bowl, combine onion, basil, salt, pepper, milk, eggs and cheese.
4. Add to skillet. Cover and cook over medium-low heat until egg mixture is almost set, 5-10 minutes.
5. Remove cover. Place skillet in oven. Broil 4 inches from heat for 1 minute, or until egg mixture is set.

Pantry Items:
Salt, Pepper, Basil, Onion, Eggs

Grocery Items:
Zucchini, Feta cheese

 Serve With:
Green Salad or sliced red tomato and whole wheat rolls.

Time: 25 minutes

BLACK BEANS AND RICE

Black beans, also called turtle beans, are a staple in Latin American cuisine.

2 Servings	Ingredients	6 Servings
½ cup	Uncooked rice	1 ½ cup
1 Tbsp	Vegetable oil	2 Tbsp
¼ cup	Bell Pepper, chopped	¾ cup
1 can (2 cups)	Canned black beans	2 cans (4 cups)
¼ cup	Water	¾ cup
1 large	Tomato, chopped	1 large
1 ½ tsp	Instant minced onion	1 Tbsp
1 ½ tsp	Chili powder	1 Tbsp
1 Tbsp	Lime juice	3 Tbsp
2 quart	Saucepan	Dutch oven

1. Cook rice according to package directions.

2. Meanwhile, in saucepan, saute bell pepper in oil over medium-low heat until crisp tender, 3-4 minutes.

3. Drain and rinse black beans. Add to saucepan with remaining ingredients.

4. Bring to boil. Reduce heat and simmer until warmed through, about 10 minutes.

5. Serve over rice.

6. Sprinkle with shredded cheese if desired.

Pantry Items:
Rice, oil, dried onion, chili powder

Grocery Items:
Bell pepper, tomato, black beans, lime juice

 Serve with: Green salad

 Cook's Tip: Don't care for bell pepper? Substitute chopped carrot, celery or zucchini.

Time: 20 minutes

WELSH RAREBIT

This dish is traditionally made with beer, but milk may be used instead if you prefer.

2 Servings	Ingredients	6 Servings
¾ cup	American or Cheddar cheese, shredded	2 ¼ cup
¼ cup	Beer	¾ cup
½ tsp	Dry mustard	1 tsp
dash	Salt	¼ tsp
dash	Ground red pepper	¼ tsp
1	Large egg	1
2 quart	Saucepan	3 quart

1. Heat cheese and beer over very low heat in a heavy saucepan stirring constantly until cheese melts and sauce is smooth, 4-5 minutes.
2. Add mustard, salt and pepper and mix well.
3. Beat egg in heat proof bowl. Stir ½ to 1 cup of hot mixture into beaten egg.
4. Return egg mixture to the remaining hot mixture in the saucepan.
5. Cook and stir constantly until mixture thickens, about 10 minutes.
6. Pour over toast or crackers and serve as is, or lightly brown under the broiler if so desired.

Pantry Items:
Salt, Red Pepper, Dry mustard, egg

 Serve With:

Sliced tomatoes and cucumbers or cooked green beans.

Grocery Items:
American cheese, beer

Time: 20 minutes

FETTUCCINE ALFREDO

Traditional Alfredo sauce is laden with butter and cream. This lighter version eliminates most of the fat while retaining the creamy taste.

2 Servings	Ingredients	6 Servings
1 Tbsp	Butter or margarine	3 Tbsp
¼ tsp	Instant minced garlic	½ tsp
½ cup	Milk	1 ½ cup
½ cup	Parmesan cheese	1 ½ cup
½ cup	Ricotta cheese	1 ½ cup
dash	Black pepper	dash
6 ounces	Fettuccine	18 ounces
2 quart	Saucepan	Dutch oven

1. Cook fettuccine according to package directions.
2. Add garlic to fettuccine and water during last 2 minutes of cooking.
3. Meanwhile, melt butter in a small bowl in the microwave.
4. Blend milk, cheeses, and melted butter in blender, or using a whisk, until smooth.
5. Add to drained fettuccine and toss to coat.
7. Garnish with ground pepper.

 Serve with:

Steamed broccoli and crusty, hard rolls.

Pantry Items:
Milk, butter dried garlic, pepper, pasta

Grocery Items:
Parmesan cheese, ricotta cheese

 Cooks Tip:

For variety, add broccoli to the cooking fettuccine. Garnish with cherry tomatoes.

Time: 20 minutes

TEX-MEX SCRAMBLED EGGS

A flavorful twist on traditional scrambled eggs. Good for brunch, lunch, or a light dinner.

2 Servings	Ingredients	6 Servings
2 Tbsp	Butter or margarine	3 Tbsp
4	Large eggs	12
2 Tbsp	Milk	6 Tbsp
1 Tbsp	Canned green chiles	3 Tbsp
1 Tbsp	Pimiento, from a jar	3 Tbsp
½ tsp	Chili powder	1 ½ tsp
¼ cup	Shredded Pepper Jack cheese	¾ cup
6 inch	Skillet	12 inch

1. Mix chiles, pimento, chili powder and cheese. Set aside.
2. Melt butter in skillet over medium heat.
3. In a small bowl, mix together eggs and milk. Pour into skillet.
4. Cook over low heat, stirring occasionally until eggs are almost cooked through, about 5 minutes.
4. Add chili mixture from step 1.
5. Stir, and continue cooking until eggs are set and mixture is heated through, 3-5 more minutes.

 Serve With:

Serve over toasted English muffins or rolled in flour tortillas with salsa and sour cream. Round out the meal by adding a green salad.

Pantry Items:
Milk, chili powder, butter, eggs

Grocery Items:
Canned pimento, pepper Jack cheese, canned green chiles

TOSS IT IN THE OVEN

Sometimes you just want to be able to fix dinner and "Toss it in the Oven" while you get other things done. The recipes in this section allow you to do just that. Most can be put together quickly with little advanced preparation, then baked for 15-50 minutes, giving you time to walk on the treadmill, read a story to your toddler, or pick up the dishes left over from breakfast. Many of these meals, like Meatloaf, Tamale Pie, and Easy, Cheesy Mac will remind you of Mom's home cooking. Others, like Vegetable Panini, Broccoli Quiche, and Chicken Enchilada Casserole, fit our more modern palates. All are perfect for a cool autumn evening, a cold snowy afternoon, or a family potluck any time of the year. "Toss it in the Oven" recipes:

★   Have a time saving twist - even the lasagna and baked beans

★   Often provide a complete meal in one dish.

★   Fit the preferences of meat eaters and vegetarians alike.

★   Make perfect leftovers for tomorrow's lunch.

★   Can be made ahead of time and baked at your convenience.

★   Are the meals you remember fondly from your childhood, and your children will remember in years to come.

★   Warm your belly and soothe your soul.

Toss It In The Oven

TOSS IT IN THE OVEN 69

Time: 60 minutes

GRETA'S FAVORITE CASSEROLE

Faced with the prospect of feeding four picky eaters on a budget, my mother was forced to be a creative cook. She invented this dish one night, while cleaning out the cupboard. It is still a family favorite.

2 Servings	Ingredients	6 Servings
4 oz (1 ½ cups)	Pasta shells	1 lb. (4 ½ cups)
⅓ lb.	Ground beef	1 lb
1 tsp	Instant minced onion	1 Tbsp
¾ cup	Tomato sauce	2 cups
½ cup	Cheddar cheese soup	1 (14 oz. can)
1 quart	Baking dish	3 quart

1. Preheat oven to 325°F.
2. Grease baking dish and set aside.
3. Cook pasta shells according to package directions, 8 minutes, or until almost done.
4. Meanwhile, brown ground beef in skillet over medium heat. Drain fat.
5. Mix drained macaroni shells, browned ground beef and remaining ingredients.
6. Turn into greased casserole. Bake for 30 - 40 minutes or until bubbly.

Pantry Items:
Dried onion, tomato sauce

Grocery Items:
Pasta shells, ground beef, soup

 Serve With: Green beans and breadsticks

 Cook's Tip: Nacho Cheese soup adds extra flavor when used in place of the Cheddar Cheese soup.

71

Time: 50 minutes

BETTER THAN A BURGER MEATLOAF

This version of our favorite comfort food includes all the usual burger trimmings.

2 Servings	Ingredients	6 Servings
1	Large egg	1
½ lb.	Ground beef	1 ½ lbs.
3 Tbsp	Bread crumbs	$^2/_3$ cup
1 tsp	Instant minced onion	1 Tbsp
½ tsp	Dried basil leaves	1 tsp
½ tsp	Instant minced garlic	1 tsp
1 tsp	Prepared mustard	1 Tbsp
1 Tbsp	Ketchup	3 Tbsp
1 Tbsp	Brown sugar	3 Tbsp
8 x 8 inch	Baking dish	9 x 13 inch

1. Preheat oven to 350°F.
2. In a large bowl, beat egg with a fork.
3. Add ground beef, bread crumbs, minced onion, basil leaves, minced garlic, and prepared mustard. Mix well.
4. Shape mixture into a loaf shape, no more than 1 ½ inches thick, on the baking dish.
5. Bake for 30 minutes.
6. Mix ketchup and brown sugar. Spread over meatloaf.
7. Return to oven and bake for 15 minutes more.

Pantry Items:
Egg, seasonings, tomato sauce, mustard, bread crumbs, ketchup, brown sugar

Grocery Items:
Ground beef

 Serve With: Mashed potatoes or baked potato wedges, green beans and crusty rolls.

Time: 45 minutes

TAMALE PIE

Tamale Pie takes the best of Mexican fare, and transforms it to a favorite American form - the casserole. Use a cheese that melts easily here, American, Cheddar, or Monterey jack are all good choices.

2 Servings	Ingredients	6 Servings
½ lb.	Ground beef	1 ½ lbs.
1 tsp	Instant minced onion	1 Tbsp
1 tsp	Chili powder	1 Tbsp
1 cup	Canned Mexican-style tomatoes	1 can (14oz)
½ cup	Frozen corn	1 ½ cups
3 Tbsp	Black olives, sliced	½ cup
½ cup	Cheese	1 ½ cups
¾ cup	Tube polenta	1 (16oz tube)
8 x 8"	Baking dish	9 x 13"

1. Preheat oven to 375°F.
2. In a skillet, brown ground beef over medium-high heat. Drain fat.
3. Add minced onion, chili powder, the tomatoes, corn and black olives to the skillet with the ground beef. Cook over medium heat until liquid evaporates.

4. Add cheese. Stir until melted.
5. Spoon into greased baking dish. Chop polenta and spread over top. Top with additional cheese if desired.
6. Bake for 30 minutes, or until bubbly. Let stand 5 minutes before serving.

Pantry Items:
Seasonings, canned tomatoes

Grocery Items:
Ground beef, corn, cheese, polenta, olives

 Serve With: Rice or warm tortillas and steamed vegetables.

Time: 60 minutes

LASAGNA

Let the oven do the work with this easy-to-prepare lasagna. The noodles cook themselves as the dish bakes. Do not pre-thaw the broccoli -it helps soften the noodles.

2 servings	Ingredients	6 Servings
$1/_3$ lb.	Ground beef	1 lb.
1 cup	Prepared pasta sauce	3 cups
1 (14oz can)	Canned tomatoes, diced	3 (14 oz. cans)
¾ cup	Frozen, chopped broccoli	2 cups
1 tsp	Instant minced onion	1 Tbsp
½ tsp	Dried oregano leaves	1 ½ tsp
1 cup	Cottage cheese	3 cups
2 Tbsp	Parmesan cheese	6 Tbsp
6	Lasagna noodles	16
¾ cup	Shredded mozzarella	2 cups
8" x 6"	Baking dish	13" x 9"

1. Preheat oven to 350°F.
2. Brown ground beef over medium-high heat. Drain fat.
3. Mix together Spaghetti sauce, diced tomatoes, frozen broccoli and dried onion. Set aside.
4. Mix together oregano, cottage cheese, and Parmesan cheese. Set aside.
5. In greased baking dish, alternate layers of sauce, noodles, ground beef, and cheese mixture, ending with noodles and sauce.
6. Top with mozzarella cheese. Bake for 45 minutes or until bubbly. Let stand for 10 minutes before serving.

Pantry Items: Canned tomatoes, seasonings

Grocery Items: Ground beef, spaghetti sauce, broccoli, cottage cheese, Parmesan cheese, lasagna noodles, mozzarella

 Serve With: Green salad and garlic bread

Time: 65 minutes

SCALLOPED HAM AND POTATOES

2 Servings	Ingredients	6 Servings
2 large (2 ½ cups)	Potatoes	6 medium (7 ½ cups)
4 slices	Sliced ham	12 slices
2 Tbsp	Flour	6 Tbsp
2 Tbsp	Butter or margarine	6 Tbsp
1 tsp	Instant minced onion	1 Tbsp
1 ¼ cup	Milk	3 ¾ cups
¾ cup	Cheddar cheese	3 cups
6 drops	Hot sauce	½ tsp
1 quart	Baking dish	3 quart

1. Preheat oven to 400ºF.

2. Peel potatoes and slice very thinly. Cut ham slices into long pieces. Set aside.

3. In a glass bowl, melt butter in the microwave. Stir in flour and dried onion. Add milk. Microwave for 2-3 minutes. Remove from microwave and stir. Return to microwave for 2-3 additional minutes. Remove from microwave and stir in cheese and hot sauce until cheese melts.

4. Spray casserole dish with nonstick cooking spray. Arrange alternate layers of potatoes, ham, and cheese sauce.

5. Bake, uncovered for 40 - 50 minutes, or until potatoes are tender.

Pantry Items:
Flour, butter, dried onion, milk, hot sauce

Grocery Items:
Potatoes, ham, cheeses

 Serve With: Green salad or steamed broccoli spears and sliced tomatoes.

☺ **Cook's Tip:** Make this dish even easier by substituting one can of cheddar cheese soup plus 2 cups of milk for the cheese sauce.

Time: 65 minutes

ORANGE PORK AND RICE

2 Servings	Ingredients	6 Servings
1 tsp	Vegetable oil	1 Tbsp
2 (¾ lbs)	Pork chops or tenderloin	6 (2 ¼ lbs)
1 cup	Quick cooking brown rice	3 cups
½ cup	Orange juice	1 ½ cups
⅓ cup	Water	1 cup
1 tsp	Prepared mustard	1 Tbsp
1 tsp	Vinegar	1 Tbsp
1 Tbsp	Brown sugar	3 Tbsp
8 x 8"	Baking dish	9 x 13"

1. Preheat oven to 350°F. Boil water.
2. Heat oil in skillet. Brown pork chops or tenderloin over medium-high heat, about 5 minutes.
3. Combine orange juice, mustard, vinegar and brown sugar.
4. Place rice in greased baking dish. Top with pork. Pour orange juice mixture over all.
5. Add boiling water. Cover and bake for 45 minutes or until done.

Pantry Items:
Oil, brown rice, mustard, vinegar, brown sugar

Serve with: Steamed broccoli or green beans.

Grocery Items:
Pork chops, orange juice

Time: 40 minutes

PACIFIC RIM SALMON

2 Servings	Ingredients	6 Servings
2	Salmon steaks (about 2" thick)	6
2 Tbsp	Melted butter or margarine	$1/_3$ cup
1 (8oz. can)	Pineapple rings	1 (16 oz. can)
1 tsp	Soy sauce	1 Tbsp
1 tsp	Brown sugar	1 Tbsp
8 x 8"	Baking dish	9 x 13"

1. Preheat oven to 350°F.
2. Place salmon steaks in baking dish.
3. Mix soy sauce, brown sugar, melted butter and pineapple juice from the canned pineapple.
4. Pour over salmon steaks. Place pineapple rings around salmon. Cover loosely with foil.
5. Bake for 25-30 minutes.

Pantry Items:
Butter, soy sauce, brown sugar

Grocery Items:
Salmon, pineapple

 Serve With: Rice pilaf and sliced tomatoes and cucumbers.

77

Time: 55 minutes

CHICKEN POT PIE

Another good way to use up leftover chicken or turkey. No leftovers?
Use packaged pre-cooked chicken or frozen, breaded chicken tenders.

2 Servings	Ingredients	6 Servings
1 medium (1 ¼ cup)	Potato	3 medium (3 ¾ cups)
1 cup	Frozen, mixed vegetables	3 cups
1 tsp	Instant minced onion	1 Tbsp
½ cup	Cooked chicken, chopped	1 ½ cups
½ (14oz. can)	Low fat cream of celery soup	1 (14oz.can)
$\frac{1}{3}$ cup	Milk	1 cup
2	Refrigerated pie crust	2
1 quart	Baking dish	3 quart

1. Preheat oven to 425°F.

2. Peel potato and cut into 1 inch pieces. Boil in small amount of water until soft, about 5 minutes.

3. Drain potato and combine with frozen vegetables, onion, chicken, soup and milk in a large bowl. Stir to mix well.

4. Arrange one pie crust in bottom of baking dish. Fill with chicken-vegetable mixture.

5. Arrange remaining pie crust over the top of the mixture. Cut slits in the pie crust to allow the release of steam.

6. Bake for 30 - 45 minutes, or until pie crust is brown and mixture is bubbly.

 Serve With: Crusty rolls

 Cook's Tip: When using a small baking dish, you may be able to use only one pie crust. Cut the crust in half and mold one half for the bottom, and the other for the top crust.

Pantry Items:
Dried onion, milk, soup

Grocery Items:
Potato, frozen vegetables, chicken, pie crust

Time: 60 minutes

OVEN BARBEQUED CHICKEN

Barbeque sauce is simple to make and much more flavorful than the packaged options. Use either bone-in or boneless chicken for this easy picnic treat.

2 Servings	Ingredients	6 Servings
1 ½ lbs.	Chicken parts	4 ½ lbs.
3 Tbsp	Ketchup	½ cup
3 Tbsp	Molasses	½ cup
2 tsp	Vinegar	2 Tbsp
1 ½ Tbsp	Prepared mustard	¼ cup
2 tsp	Brown sugar	2 Tbsp
6 drops	Hot pepper sauce (optional)	½ tsp
8 x 8"	Baking dish	9 x 13"

1. Preheat oven to 450°F.
2. Skin chicken. Rinse and pat dry.
3. Arrange chicken in baking dish. Bake for 20 minutes.
4. Meanwhile, in a small bowl, mix ketchup, molasses, vinegar, mustard, brown sugar and hot pepper sauce. Pour over chicken.
5. Continue baking for 15-30 minutes, or until chicken is cooked through.

Pantry Items:
Ketchup, molasses, vinegar, mustard, brown sugar, hot pepper sauce

Grocery Items:
Chicken

 Serve With:
Potato salad and Three Bean salad

79

Time: 50 minutes

CHICKEN BITES AND SWEET POTATO CHIPS

A nutritious, and delicious, alternative to fast food chicken and fries.

2 Servings	Ingredients	6 Servings
2 large	Sweet potatoes	6 large
3 Tbsp	Butter or margarine	$^2/_3$ cup
½ tsp	Lemon-pepper seasoning	1 ½ tsp
½ lb.	Boneless, skinless chicken breasts or tenders	1 ½ lbs
$^1/_3$ cup	Bread crumbs	1 cup
12 x 13"	Baking sheet	10 x 15"

1. Preheat oven to 400°F. In a small bowl, melt butter or margarine in the microwave.
2. Peel potatoes and cut into thin rounds. Brush with melted butter. Sprinkle with ½ of the lemon-pepper seasoning. Place potatoes on baking sheet and put in oven.
3. Cut chicken into 1 inch pieces.
4. In a plastic zipper bag, combine the bread crumbs and remaining lemon-pepper seasoning.
5. Roll chicken pieces in melted butter. Add to bag. Shake to coat.
6. Remove chicken pieces from bag and place on baking sheet with potatoes. Return to oven.
7. Bake for 20 - 30 minutes, or until chicken is no longer pink.

Pantry Items:
Butter, lemon-pepper, bread crumbs

 Serve With:

Prepared mustard or Ranch dressing for dipping. Sliced cucumbers and carrot sticks.

Grocery Items:
Chicken, sweet potatoes

Time: 50 minutes

GRAM'S CHICKEN AND RICE CASSEROLE

My husband's grandmother was a wonderful person, and an excellent cook. She prepared hearty meals that satisfied her many sons and grandsons as they worked on the family farm. Her chicken and rice combination is still my favorite.

2 Servings	Ingredients	6 Servings
½ cup	Uncooked rice	1 ½ cups
1 stalk (⅓ cup)	Celery	3 stalks (1 cup)
¾ cup	Cooked chicken	2 ¼ cups
2 Tbsp	Butter or margarine	6 Tbsp
1 tsp	Instant minced onion	1 Tbsp
2 Tbsp	Flour	6 Tbsp
1 cup	Chicken broth	3 cups
½ cup	Crushed crackers	1 cup
¼ cup	Cheese	½ cup
8 x 8"	Baking dish	9 x 13"

1. Cook rice according to package directions.
2. Preheat oven to 350ºF. Grease baking dish and set aside.
3. Chop celery and chicken.
4. In a large bowl, melt butter or margarine in microwave. Add chopped celery, dried onion and flour to melted butter. Stir in chicken broth.
5. Microwave on high setting for 2-3 minutes. Stir. Continue cooking for an additional 2-4 minutes or until sauce has thickened.
6. Mix together cooked rice, chicken, and the thickened celery-onion sauce. Spoon into baking dish. Top with crushed crackers. Sprinkle cheese over the crackers.
7. Bake, uncovered for 20 - 30 minutes or until bubbly.

Pantry Items:
Rice, butter, dried onion, flour, broth

Grocery Items:
Celery, chicken, crackers, cheese

 Serve With:

Steamed green vegetables and sliced tomatoes.

81

Time: 30 minutes

CHICKEN ENCHILADA CASSEROLE

An easy way to make everyone's favorite enchiladas.

2 Servings	Ingredients	6 Servings
1 cup	Cooked chicken	3 cups
4	Corn tortillas	12
1 cup (½ -14oz can)	Canned black beans, drained	3 cups (1 ½ 14oz cans)
1 Tbsp	Canned green chiles, diced	3 Tbsp
1 cup	Pepper-Jack cheese, shredded	3 cups
1 tsp	Instant minced onion	1 Tbsp
1 cup	Canned enchilada sauce	3 cups
2 Tbsp	Cheddar cheese	¼ cup
1 quart	Baking dish	3 quart

1. Preheat oven to 375°F. Chop or shred chicken.
2. Grease baking dish. Place half of the corn tortillas in bottom of dish.
3. In a bowl, mix together drained beans, chiles, Pepper-Jack cheese and onion. Spoon mixture over tortillas.
4. Top with remaining tortillas. Pour enchilada sauce over the top of tortillas and sprinkle with Cheddar cheese.
5. Bake for 15 - 20 minutes or until cheese melts and mixture is bubbly.

 Serve With:

Mexican rice and steamed zucchini and tomatoes.

Pantry Items:
Dried onion

Grocery Items:
Tortillas, chicken, chiles, cheeses, enchilada sauce, black beans

Time: 45 minutes

TURKEY TETRAZZINI

Add hot sauce to taste if desired.

2 Servings	Ingredients	6 Servings
4 oz.	Spaghetti pasta	12 oz.
2 Tbsp	Butter or margarine	6 Tbsp
2 Tbsp	Flour	6 Tbsp
1 ½ cup	Milk	4 ½ cups
dash	Black pepper	¼ tsp
¼ cup	Parmesan cheese	¾ cup
1 cup	Cooked turkey, chopped	3 cups
½ cup	Frozen peas	1 ½ cups
¼ cup	Canned mushrooms, drained	¾ cup
2 Tbsp	Pimiento, from a jar	6 Tbsp
8 x 8"	Baking dish	9 x 13"

1. Preheat oven to 425°F. Grease baking dish and set aside.
2. Prepare spaghetti according to package directions, drain.
3. Meanwhile, in a large bowl, melt butter in the microwave. Stir in flour and milk. Microwave on high setting for 2-3 minutes. Stir. Return to microwave for 3-4 minutes longer, or until slightly thickened.
4. Add pepper and all but 2 tablespoons of Parmesan cheese to the thickened sauce.
5. Stir drained spaghetti, cooked turkey, peas, mushrooms and pimiento into sauce. Mix well and spoon into greased baking dish.
6. Sprinkle with reserved cheese and bake for 10 -20 minutes or until bubbly.

Pantry Items:
Butter, flour, milk, pepper

Grocery Items:
Pasta, turkey, cheese, mushrooms, pimento, peas

 Serve With:

Green beans and garlic bread

83

Time: 50 minutes

TURKEY STUFFING BAKE

A great way to use up leftover holiday turkey or chicken.

2 Servings	Ingredients	6 Servings
1 stalk($^{1}/_{3}$ cup)	Celery	3 stalks (1 cup)
1 large(¼ cup)	Carrot	3 large (¾ cup)
¾ cup	Cooked turkey	2 ¼ cup
1 tsp	Dried onion	1 Tbsp
½ cup	Frozen peas	1 ½ cups
1 cup	Seasoned stuffing mix	3 cups
½ (14oz. can)	Low-fat cream of celery soup	1 ½ (14oz. can)
¼ cup	Milk	¾ cup
1 quart	Baking dish	3 quart

1. Preheat oven to 350°F. Grease baking dish and set aside.
2. Chop celery, carrot and turkey.
3. Mix together celery, carrot, turkey, onion, peas, stuffing mix, soup and milk Spoon into the greased baking dish.
4. Bake, covered, for 30 - 40 minutes or until bubbly.

Pantry Items:
Dried onion, milk, soup

Grocery Items:
Celery, carrot, stuffing mix, turkey, peas,

 Serve With:

Whole cranberry sauce

Time: 45 minutes

EASY CHEESY MAC

Throw away the box! Real, homemade macaroni and cheese is a true taste treat, and not very difficult to make. It is the perfect way to use up odds and ends of different cheeses.

2 Servings	Ingredients	6 Servings
1 cup	Elbow macaroni	3 cups
½	Bell Pepper	1
2 (½ cup)	Carrots	6 (1 ½ cups)
1 tsp	Instant minced onion	1 Tbsp
2 Tbsp	Butter or margarine	6 Tbsp
2 Tbsp	Flour	6 Tbsp
1 ¼ cup	Milk	3 ¾ cup
½ tsp	Paprika	1 ½ tsp
2 tsp	Prepared mustard	2 Tbsp
1 cup	Shredded cheese	3 cups
6 drops	Hot sauce	½ tsp
½ cup	Bread or cracker crumbs	¾ cup
1 quart	Baking Dish	3 quart

1. Preheat oven to 350°F. Cook macaroni in boiling water for 5 minutes or until almost done.

2. Meanwhile, dice bell pepper and carrots.

3. Melt margarine in casserole dish in the microwave. Add vegetables and onion and microwave 1 minute.

4. Add flour and paprika to vegetable mixture and stir to coat vegetables. Add milk and stir.

5. Microwave on high heat for 2-3 minutes. Remove from microwave and stir. Return to microwave and continue cooking 2-3 more minutes or until mixture is thickened.

6. Add cheese, prepared mustard, and hot sauce. Stir until cheese is melted. Add drained macaroni and mix thoroughly. Top with bread or cracker crumbs.

7. Bake for 20 - 30 minutes or until browned and bubbly.

Pantry Items:
Pasta, seasonings, mustard, bread crumbs

Grocery Items:
Bell pepper, carrots, cheese

🍽 Serve With: Any simple meat dish or baked beans. Add a green salad or side of steamed broccoli.

Time: 50 minutes

FANCY BAKED BEANS

Growing up in New England, Saturday was baked beans night. Mom would get up in the morning and start the day long cooking process for that evening's feast. I still love baked beans, but save myself lots of time with this easy-to-prepare version.

2 Servings	Ingredients	6 Servings
1 small (1 ½ cups)	Canned baked beans	1 ½ large (4 ½ cups)
2 Tbsp	Honey barbeque sauce	6 Tbsp
1 tsp	Instant minced onion	1 Tbsp
$\frac{1}{8}$ tsp	Ground ginger	¼ tsp
1 ½ tsp	Prepared mustard	1 ½ Tbsp
2	Low fat or vegetarian frankfurters	6
1 quart	Baking dish	3 quart

1. Preheat oven to 325°F.
2. Cut frankfurters into 1 inch pieces.
3. Mix all ingredients together. Spoon into the baking dish.
4. Cover and bake for 30 - 45 minutes, or until beans are bubbly.
5. Served hot or cold.

 Serve With:

Baked sweet potatoes and a green salad.

 Cook's Tip:

Alter this easy dish by using different flavored baked beans and barbeque sauce.
   Don't care for barbeque sauce? Substitute jerk sauce, apple sauce or tomato sauce.

Pantry Items:
Seasonings, prepared mustard

Grocery Items:
Canned beans, barbeque sauce, frankfurters

Time: 45 minutes

ZUCCHINI - RICE CASSEROLE

A filling side dish, or a main course for the vegetarians in the family.

2 Servings	Ingredients	6 Servings
¾ cup	Quick cooking brown rice	2 ¼ cups
¾ cup	Chicken broth	2 ½ cup
1	Large eggs	2
1 small	Zucchini	2 large
1 tsp	Instant minced onion	1 Tbsp
½ tsp	Instant minced garlic	1 ½ tsp
½ cup	Feta cheese	1 ½ cups
$^1/_3$ cup	Sour cream	1 cup
8 x 8"	Baking dish	9 x 13"

1. Preheat oven to 350°F.
2. Cook rice, following package directions and using chicken broth in place of water. Grease baking dish and set aside.
3. Chop zucchini in ½" pieces.
4. Lightly beat eggs with fork. Add all ingredients, including rice.
5. Spoon mixture into a greased baking dish.
6. Bake 20 - 30 minutes, or until bubbly. Let sit 5 minutes before serving.

Pantry Items:
Seasonings, rice, eggs, broth

Grocery Items:
Feta cheese, sour cream, zucchini

 Serve With:
Pork chops or ham steak, green beans and cranberry relish.

87

Time: 45 minutes

VEGETARIAN PANINI

A tangy twist on the traditional sandwich - plus no dirty dishes!

2 Servings	Ingredients	6 Servings
2 (8 inch)	Cheese flavored prepared pizza crusts	6 (8 inch)
4 slices	Provolone cheese	12 slices
½ cup	Roasted red pepper	1 ½ cup
2 Tbsp	Sun dried tomatoes	$^1/_3$ cup
1 cup	Sliced zucchini	3 cups
2 tsp	Balsamic vinegar	2 Tbsp
dash	Pepper	¼ tsp
	Foil	

1. Preheat oven to 300°F.
2. Slice each crust in half, lengthwise. Finely chop broccoli or zucchini. Slice tomatoes and red pepper.
3. Layer one crust half with cheese slices and vegetables.
4. Drizzle with vinegar and sprinkle with pepper.
5. Repeat steps 3 and 4 with remaining halves for two or six servings.
6. Top with remaining crust half. Wrap each in foil.
7. Bake for 30 minutes.

 Serve With:

Tomato soup or coleslaw.

 Cook's Tip: Add fresh basil and sliced ham or turkey if desired.

Pantry Items:
Vinegar, pepper

Grocery Items:
Pizza crusts, cheese, lettuce, red pepper, tomatoes, broccoli or zucchini

Time: 60 minutes

BROCCOLI QUICHE

Excellent for brunch or a light Sunday dinner.

2 Servings	Ingredients	6 Servings
1	Refrigerated or frozen pie crust	1
1 cup	Frozen hash brown potatoes	2 ½ cups
1 tsp	Instant minced onion	1 Tbsp
1 cup	Frozen, chopped broccoli	2 ½ cups
2 Tbsp	Sun-dried tomatoes	⅓ cup
½ cup	Parmesan cheese	1 ½ cups
2	Large eggs	6
½ cup	Milk	1 ½ cups
1	Fresh tomatoes	2
8 inch	Pie plate	12 inch

1. Thaw hash browns and broccoli. Slice sun-dried tomatoes.
2. Preheat oven to 450°F.
3. If using a refrigerated pie crust, place in pie plate according to package directions.
4. Line pastry shell with foil, and cook for 8 minutes.
5. Remove pastry shell from oven and reduce heat to 325°. Remove foil.
6. Beat eggs lightly with a fork. Add remaining ingredients except fresh tomato.
7. Poor mixture into pastry shell. Slice tomatoes and layer around edges of quiche.
8. Bake for 35-45 minutes, or until knife inserted in center comes out clean.
9. Let sit for 10 minutes before serving.

Pantry Items:
Dried onion, milk, eggs

Grocery Items:
Pie crust, hash browns, broccoli, sun dried tomatoes, tomatoes

 Serve With:

Crusty bread, crisp bacon, and a green salad.

89

Time: 50 minutes

RATATOUILLE BAKE

The perfect way to use up summer's abundance of squash.

2 Servings	Ingredients	6 Servings
1 large	Zucchini	3 large
1 small	Bell Peppers	2 large
½ large	Eggplant	1 large
1	Summer squash	3
½ tsp	Dried basil leaves	1 ½ tsp
¼ tsp	Black pepper	½ tsp
1 tsp	Instant minced onion	1 Tbsp
1 cup (8oz can)	Canned tomatoes, diced	3 cups (1 ½, 14oz cans)
½ cup	Seasoned stuffing mix	3 cups
½ cup	Shredded cheddar cheese	¾ cup
1 quart	Baking Dish	3 quart

1. Preheat oven to 350°F. Grease baking dish and set aside.
2. Cut zucchini, bell pepper, eggplant, and summer squash into 3/4"
pieces. In a separate glass bowl, microwave on high setting four minutes.
3. Mix vegetables with basil leaves, black pepper, minced onion,
tomatoes, and stuffing mix. Turn into greased baking dish.
4. Cover and bake for 30 minutes, stirring once during cooking time.
5. Remove cover and top casserole with cheese. Return to oven.
6. Continue cooking until cheese has
melted and casserole is bubbly, about 5
more minutes.

 Serve With:

Grilled chicken breasts.

 Cook's Tip: Use a cubed, bread
stuffing mix for this casserole. Crushed
stuffing does not hold up well with the liquid.

Pantry Items:
Seasonings, canned
tomatoes

Grocery Items:
Zucchini, bell pepper,
eggplant, summer
squash, cheese,
stuffing mix

ONE POT MEALS

When I get home from a long day at work, the last thing I want to deal with is a sink full of dirty dishes. And I find that as the week progresses, my interest in fixing new, modern tasting meals wanes. By Thursday night, I am ready for some old familiar favorites. *One Pot Meals* are the perfect solution, providing delicious, nutritious dinners, while keeping the sink practically empty. In this section you will find:

* Satisfying soups for cold winter evenings.

* Quick and easy salads and sandwiches.

* Creamy pastas, hearty stews, favorite Asian and Cajun specialties.

* Kids' favorites.

* Dinners that are perfect served as is, or can be rounded out with rolls and steamed vegetables.

* The perfect way to use up odds and ends of frozen and fresh vegetables.

One Pot Meals

ONE POT MEALS...................... 91

Time: 30 minutes

SZECHWAN BEEF

Another restaurant favorite made easily at home.

2 Servings	Ingredients	6 Servings
1 oz.	Cellophane noodles	3 ounces
½ lb.	Top round steak	1 ½ lbs.
3 cups	Bok choy	9 cups
½ cup	Bell Pepper	1 ½ cups
1 Tbsp	Vegetable oil	3 Tbsp
½ cup	Canned baby corn	1 ½ cups
1 ½ tsp	Soy sauce	1 ½ Tbsp
¼ tsp	Ground ginger	½ tsp
¼ tsp	Crushed red pepper	½ tsp
1 Tbsp	Hoisin sauce	3 Tbsp
1 tsp	Cornstarch	1 tsp
8 inch	Skillet	12 inch

1. Place noodles in a large bowl and cover with boiling water. Let sit for 20 minutes. Drain.

2. Meanwhile, thinly slice beef, chop bok choy and bell pepper.

3. Heat oil in skillet over medium-high heat. Stir-fry the beef 3-4 minutes or until no longer pink. Remove from skillet.

4. Reduce heat to medium. Add corn and bell pepper to skillet. Stir fry 3-5 minutes. Add bok choy. Cover and cook 4-5 minutes, or until bok choy leaves have wilted and stem pieces are tender.

5. Return beef to skillet. Combine soy sauce, ginger, red pepper, hoisin sauce, and cornstarch with 3 tablespoons of water.

6. Add sauce mixture and drained noodles to skillet. Cook and stir until slightly thick, 2-3 minutes.

Pantry Items:
Oil, soy sauce, seasonings, cornstarch

Grocery Items:
Cellophane noodles, baby corn, bell pepper, bok choy, beef, hoisin sauce

 Serve With:
Purchased egg rolls and fortune cookies.

93

Time: 65 minutes

TOMATO BEEF STEW

This has been my favorite beef stew since I was a little girl. The tomato sauce and red wine add a touch of sweetness to the vegetables.

2 Servings	Ingredients	6 Servings
½ lb.	Stew beef	1 ½ lbs.
1 large (¼ cup)	Carrots	3 large (¾ cup)
2 small (1 ½ cups)	Potatoes	6 small (4 ½ cups)
1 ½ tsp	Vegetable oil	1 ½ Tbsp
cup	Tomato sauce	2 cups
¼ cup	Dry red wine	¾ cup
¼ cup	Water	¾ cup
1 tsp	Instant minced onion	1 Tbsp
½ tsp	Instant minced garlic	1 ½ tsp
1	Bay leaf	1
¼ tsp	Dried thyme leaves	¾ tsp
1 ½ tsp	Cornstarch	1 ½ tsp
cup	Fresh mushrooms	1 cup
cup	Peas	1 cup
2 quart	Saucepan	Dutch oven

1. Cut stew beef into bite-sized pieces. Chop carrots and peel and chop potatoes into 1 inch pieces. Set aside.

2. Add oil to saucepan. Brown beef in saucepan over medium-high heat, about 5 minutes.

3. Add tomato sauce, red wine, water, carrots, potatoes and seasonings. Bring to boil. Reduce heat to medium-low. Cover and simmer for 30 - 40 minutes.

4. Mix cornstarch with 3 Tbsp water. Add to saucepan along with mushrooms and peas.

5. Cook and stir for 10 more minutes or until mushrooms are tender and sauce has thickened. Remove bay leaf before serving.

Pantry Items:
Oil, seasonings, cornstarch, tomato sauce

Grocery Items:
Stewing beef, red wine, carrots, potatoes, mushrooms, peas.

 Serve With:

Rolls or crackers

Time: 35 minutes

CHILI

Pass additional chili powder for those who like their chili extra spicy.

2 Servings	Ingredients	6 Servings
½ lb.	Ground beef	1 ½ lbs.
1 (14oz. can)	Canned red kidney beans	3 (14oz. cans)
1 large (¼ cup)	Carrots	3 large (¾ cup)
1 Tbsp	Instant minced onion	3 Tbsp
1 tsp	Instant minced garlic	1 Tbsp
2 tsp	Chili powder	2 Tbsp
¼ cup	Tomato paste	¾ cup
2 cups	Water	6 cups
2 Tbsp	Flour	6 Tbsp
½ cup	Frozen corn	1 ½ cups
2 quart	Saucepan	Dutch oven

1. Brown the ground beef in the saucepan over medium-high heat, about 5 minutes. Drain fat.
2. Chop the carrots and drain and rinse the kidney beans.
3. Add all ingredients to the ground beef in the saucepan.
4. Bring to a boil. Reduce heat to medium-low. Cover and simmer until flavors are well mingled, about 20 minutes. Stir occasionally.

Pantry Items:
Seasonings, tomato paste, flour, kidney beans

Grocery Items:
Ground beef, carrots, corn.

 Serve With:

Crackers

Time:50 minutes

EASY BEEF AND MACARONI POT

A new twist on that cafeteria favorite, American Chop Suey, with an updated taste and bursting with vegetables.

2 Servings	Ingredients	6 Servings
¼ lb	Ground beef	¾ lb.
2 cups	Beef broth	6 cups
½ cup	Canned mushrooms, drained	1 ½ cup
1 ½ tsp	Instant minced onion	1 ½ Tbsp
½ tsp	Instant minced garlic	1 ½ tsp
¼ cup	Tomato paste	¾ cup
1 (14oz can)	Italian-Style stewed tomatoes	3 (14oz. cans)
1 ¼ cups	Elbow macaroni	3 ¾ cups
1 cup	Frozen broccoli (optional)	3 cups
2 quart	Saucepan	Dutch oven

1. Sauté ground beef over medium heat until brown, about 5 minutes. Drain fat.

2. Stir in broth, mushrooms, onion, garlic, tomato paste, and stewed tomatoes, breaking tomatoes up with a spoon. Bring to a boil.

3. Add elbows, stirring constantly. Return to boiling.

4. Reduce heat to medium. Boil gently, stirring often, until elbows are almost cooked through, 15 - 20 minutes.

5. Add frozen broccoli. Continue cooking until elbows are tender and broccoli is warmed through. Cover and let sit 5 minutes before serving.

Pantry Items:
Seasonings, tomato paste, pasta, broth

Grocery Items:
Mushrooms, stewed tomatoes, broccoli

 Serve With:

Garlic Bread

Time: 45 minutes

STEVE'S JAMBALAYA

This recipe was developed by my husband and is a favorite of my sons and their friends. The servings are hearty, and any leftovers taste even better the next day.

2 Servings	Ingredients	6 Servings
½ cup	Bell Pepper	1 ½ cups
1 large (¼ cup)	Carrots	3 large (¾ cup)
½ lb	Smoked sausage	1 ½ lbs.
1 tsp.	Vegetable oil	1 Tbsp.
1 tsp	Instant minced onion	1 Tbsp
1 tsp	Cajun seasoning	1 Tbsp
¼ cup	Tomato paste	¾ cup
2 ½ cups	Water	7 ½ cups
1 cup	Canned red kidney beans, drained	3 cups
¼ cup	Frozen corn	¾ cups
½ cup	Uncooked rice	1 ½ cup
2 quart	Saucepan	Dutch oven

1. Chop bell pepper and carrots. Slice sausage into ½ inch pieces.
2. Heat oil in saucepan over medium heat. Add sausage and bell pepper and sauté until pepper is tender, 4-5 minutes.

3. Add all remaining ingredients to saucepan. Bring to a boil. Reduce heat to medium-low.
4. Cover and simmer until rice and carrots are tender and liquid is absorbed, 15 - 20 minutes.
5. Let stand 10 minutes before serving.

Pantry Items:
Dried onion, tomato paste, rice, Cajun seasoning, kidney beans

Grocery Items:
Sausage, bell pepper, corn, carrots

 Serve With:

Crusty rolls

Time: 25 minutes

CHEESY HAM AND PASTA

Use a medium shaped pasta for this dish, like bow ties, wagon wheels or rotini.

2 Servings	Ingredients	6 Servings
6 oz.	Pasta	1 ½ lbs.
½ cup	Frozen peas or asparagus	1 ½ cups
½ cup	Cooked ham	1 ½ cups
2 Tbsp	Roasted red pepper	6 Tbsp
½ cup	Half and Half	1 ½ cups
½ cup	Parmesan cheese	1 ½ cups
1 Tbsp	Butter or margarine	3 Tbsp
4 drops	Hot sauce	¼ tsp
2 quart	Saucepan	Dutch oven

1. Cook pasta according to package directions. Add frozen peas or asparagus during the last 5 minutes.
2. While pasta is cooking, dice ham and slice red pepper into strips.
3. Drain pasta and vegetables. Return to saucepan.
4. Add all ingredients to the saucepan. Toss gently until cheese is melted and pasta is coated with sauce, 3-5 minutes.
5. Serve immediately

 Serve With:

Crusty rolls

 Cook's Tip:

Roasted red pepper can be found in the pickle aisle of your grocers.

Pantry Items:
Butter, pasta

Grocery Items:
Vegetables, ham, half and half, Parmesan cheese

Time:25 minutes

WARM NICOISE SALAD

Nicoise salad originates from Nice, on the French Riviera.

2 Servings	Ingredients	6 Servings
1 cup	Small red potatoes	3 cups
1 cup	Frozen green beans	3 cups
4 cups	Romaine lettuce, chopped	12 cups
1	Tomato	3
¼ cup	Black olives	¾ cup
2 slices	Red onion	6 slices
1 (3oz. can)	Water packed tuna, drained	2 (6oz cans)
½ cup	Purchased Italian salad dressing	1 cup
1 quart	Saucepan	2 quart

1. Cut potatoes into quarters. Place in saucepan with enough water to cover. Bring to a boil over medium-high heat. Reduce heat to medium and cook 10 to 12 minutes, or until tender.

2. Add green beans to potatoes during last 3-4 minutes.

3. Meanwhile chop lettuce, cut tomatoes into wedges, slice olives and red onion and layer in large salad bowl. Break tuna into large pieces and set aside.

4. Drain potatoes and green beans. Toss with half of the salad dressing. Place on top of the salad mixture. Top with the tuna. Drizzle remaining dressing over salad. Serve immediately.

Pantry Items:
None

Grocery Items:
Potatoes, beans, lettuce, tomato, olives, onion, tuna, salad dressing

 Serve With:

Warm garlic bread

Time: 40 minutes

TROPICAL CHICKEN

A quick, light meal sure to satisfy on a hot summer evening.

2 Servings	Ingredients	6 Servings
1	Sweet potato	3
½ cup	Bell Pepper	1 ½ cup
1 cup	Mango	3 cups
½ lb.	Chicken tenders	1 ½ lbs.
1 ½ tsp	Vegetable oil	1 Tbsp
dash	Ground red pepper	¼ tsp
1 cup	Coconut milk	3 cups
½ cup	Water	1 ½ cup
1	Banana	3
1 cup	Quick-cooking brown rice	3 cups
2 quart	Saucepan	Dutch oven

1. Peel sweet potato and cut into one inch pieces. Chop bell pepper. Cut mango into 3/4 inch chunks.

2. Heat oil in saucepan over medium-high heat. Add chicken tenders and brown, about 3 minutes. Reduce heat to medium.

3. Add sweet potatoes, bell pepper, mango, red pepper, coconut milk and water to the saucepan. Cover and cook until vegetables are tender, stirring occasionally, about 15 minutes.

4. Add rice and bananas to saucepan. Increase heat to medium-high. Bring to boil. Reduce heat to medium-low. Cover and simmer 5 minutes. Remove saucepan from heat and let sit 5 minutes before serving.

Pantry Items:
 Oil, rice, red pepper

Grocery Items:
Chicken, sweet potato, bell pepper, mango, banana, coconut milk

 Serve With:

Sliced cucumber and tomatoes.

 Cook's Tip: If mango is unavailable, use papaya, peaches, or plums.

Time: 40 minutes

CREAMY CHICKEN

Use orange or red bell pepper to enhance the eye-appeal of this dish.

2 Servings	Ingredients	6 Servings
½ cup	Bell Pepper	1 ½ cups
1 Tbsp	Vegetable oil	2 Tbsp
2	Boneless, skinless chicken breasts	6
¼ tsp	Lemon-pepper seasoning	¾ tsp
1 cup	Small pasta shells or orzo	3 tsp
½ (14 oz. can)	Low-fat cream of celery soup	1 ½ (14oz cans)
1 cup	Chicken broth	3 cups
1 cup	Frozen whole green beans	3 cups
8 inch	Skillet	12 inch

1. Slice bell pepper.

2 Heat oil in skillet over medium heat. Add chicken breasts and brown on each side, about 2 minutes each.

3. Add bell pepper, lemon-pepper seasoning, pasta, soup and broth to the skillet. Stir to mix. Bring to a boil. Reduce heat to medium-low.

3. Cover and simmer, stirring occasionally, until pasta is nearly tender, 15 - 20 minutes. Add green beans to skillet.

4. Continue cooking until beans are warmed and chicken is cooked through, 5 more minutes.

Pantry Items:
Oil, pasta, soup

Grocery Items:
Chicken, green beans, salad dressing, bell pepper

 Serve With:

Crusty rolls and a green salad.

101

Time:30 minutes

BARBEQUE CHICKEN RAGOÛT

A ragoût is the French version of a stew.

2 Servings	Ingredients	6 Servings
1 ¼ cups	Cooked chicken	3 ¾ cups
1 stalk ($\frac{1}{3}$ cup)	Celery	3 stalks (1 cup)
2 cups	Frozen mixed stew vegetables	6 cups
1 cup	Tomato sauce	3 cups
¼ cup	Barbeque sauce	¾ cup
1 cup	Water	3 cups
2 quart	Saucepan	Dutch oven

1. Chop the chicken and slice the celery.

2. Add all ingredients to saucepan. Bring to boil over medium-high heat. Reduce heat to medium-low.

3. Cover and simmer for 20 minutes stirring occasionally, or until vegetables are cooked through.

Pantry Items:
Tomato sauce

Grocery Items:
Chicken, vegetables, celery, barbeque sauce

 Serve With:

Crusty rolls

Time: 40 minutes

SKILLET CHICKEN AND RICE

2 Servings	Ingredients	6 Servings
1 Tbsp	Vegetable oil	2 Tbsp
½ lb	Chicken tenders	1 ½ lbs.
1 cup	Water	3 cups
¾ cup	Uncooked rice	2 ¼ cups
1 (14oz.can)	Low-fat cream of celery soup	3 (14oz. cans)
½ cup	Frozen peas	1 ½ cups
1 Tbsp	Pimiento, from a jar	3 Tbsp
1 tsp	Instant minced onion	1 Tbsp
8 inch	Skillet	12 inch

1. Heat oil in skillet over medium-high heat.
2. Add chicken tenders and quickly brown both sides, 4-5 minutes.
3. Add remaining ingredients. Bring to boil. Reduce heat to medium-low.
4. Cover skillet and let simmer until rice is done, 20-25 minutes. Stir occasionally while cooking.

 Serve With:

Cranberry sauce or relish and steamed carrots

Pantry Items:
Oil, rice, dried onion, soup

Grocery Items:
Chicken, pimento, peas

 Cook's Tip:

Use frozen broccoli, green beans, or asparagus instead of peas if you like. Roasted red pepper or chopped carrots can be added in place of the pimento.

103

Time:20 minutes

CHICKEN NOODLE SOUP

Homemade soup has much more flavor than the canned variety, and is easy to prepare.

2 Servings	Ingredients	6 Servings
3 cups	Chicken broth	9 cups
1 tsp	Instant minced onion	1 Tbsp
½ tsp	Instant minced garlic	1 ½ tsp
1	Bay Leaf	1
¾ tsp	Dried marjoram	2 tsp
½ tsp	Dried thyme leaves	1 tsp
3 drops	Hot pepper sauce	¼ tsp
1 cup	Frozen mixed vegetables	3 cups
½ cup	Egg noodles	1 ½ cups
1 cup	Cooked chicken, chopped	3 cups
2 quart	Saucepan	Dutch oven

1. Combine all ingredients in the saucepan except the noodles and chicken. Bring to boil over medium-high heat.
2. Add noodles and chicken to the saucepan.
3. Reduce heat to medium-low. Cover and simmer until noodles are tender, 10 - 15 minutes.
4. Remove bay leaf before serving.

 Serve With:

Crackers or bread sticks

Pantry Items:
Seasonings, broth

 Cook's Tip:

Substitute cheese tortellini or another small pasta for the noodles if desired.

Grocery Items:
Chicken, vegetables

Time: 10 minutes

TURKEY WRAPS

The kids won't balk at dinner when you serve them this unusual wrap,
filled with their favorite foods.

2 Servings	Ingredients	6 Servings
2 slices	Bacon	6 slices
1 cup	Chopped cooked turkey or	3 cups
4 slices	Deli turkey	12 slices
2 leaves	Lettuce	6 leaves
2 slices	Provolone cheese	6 slices
½ cup	Canned mandarin orange segments, drained	1 ½ cup
2 tsp.	Peanut butter (optional)	2 Tbsp
2 tsp.	Honey mustard	2 Tbsp
2	Sandwich wraps	6
6 inch	Skillet	6 inch

1. Fry bacon in skillet until well done, about 5 minutes. Drain on paper towels.
2. Spread each wrap thinly with peanut butter. Spread with honey mustard.
3. Top each wrap with one slice of cheese, two slices or ½ cup of chicken or turkey, lettuce leaf, bacon slice and ¼ cup mandarin orange segments.
4. Wrap sandwich, securing with 2 toothpicks.

Pantry Items:
Peanut butter, mustard

Grocery Items:
Bacon, chicken or turkey, lettuce, cheese, Mandarin orange segments

 Serve With:

Purchased pasta salad or coleslaw

Time: 20 minutes

CHEF'S SALAD

The perfect meal for a hot summer day. Even small children love this salad.

2 Servings	Ingredients	6 Servings
2	Eggs	6
1	Tomatoes	3
½ cup	Cucumber	1 ½ cups
$\frac{1}{8}$ cup	Cooked ham	1 cup
$\frac{1}{8}$ cup	Cooked chicken	1 cup
$\frac{1}{8}$ cup	Cheese	1 cup
3 cups	Lettuce mix	9 cups
1 cup	Shredded cabbage and carrot mix	3 cups
¼ cup	Black olives	¾ cup

1. Hard boil the eggs (see basic recipes section). Set aside to cool.
2. Cut tomatoes into wedges. Slice cucumbers and chop ham, chicken, and cheese. (Cheese may be shredded if you prefer). Set aside.
3. Toss the lettuce mix and shredded cabbage in a large bowl.
4. Top lettuce-cabbage mix with olives, tomatoes, cucumber, meats and cheese.
5. Slice or chop peeled egg and place on top.

 Serve With:

Your favorite salad dressings and bread sticks.

 Cook's Tip:

Using a pre-packaged lettuce mix and cabbage and carrot mix from your grocers makes this quick meal even faster. Add peas, garbanzo beans, artichoke hearts and sunflower seeds for a heartier meal.

Pantry Items:
Eggs

Grocery Items:
Vegetables, meats, cheese

Time: 20 minutes

PASTA PRIMAVERA

Use your favorite pasta shape here.

2 Servings	Ingredients	6 Servings
½ lb.	Pasta	1 ½ lbs.
1 cup	Frozen broccoli, yellow squash mix	3 cups
½ cup	Frozen peas	1 ½ cups
1 cup	Canned tomatoes, diced	3 cups
½ tsp	Dried basil leaves	1 ½ tsp
¼ tsp	Crushed red pepper	¾ tsp
2 Tbsp	Parmesan cheese	6 Tbsp
2 quart	Saucepan	Dutch oven

1. Cook pasta according to package directions.
2. Add frozen vegetables during last 5 minutes of cooking.
3. Drain pasta-vegetable mix, retaining ½ cup of the pasta water. Return to pot.
4. Add tomatoes, basil, pepper and retained pasta water to pot. Heat over low heat until warmed through, about 5 minutes.
5. Top each serving with grated Parmesan cheese.

 Serve With:

Rolls

Pantry Items:
Canned tomatoes, seasonings, pasta

Grocery Items:
Frozen vegetables, Parmesan cheese

Time: 25 minutes

PASTA WITH FRESH MOZZARELLA

This dish is especially good in the summer, when the tomatoes are vine-ripe. Make it even more colorful by adding sliced black olives.

2 Servings	Ingredients	6 Servings
1 cup	Cherry tomatoes	3 cups
1 ½ Tbsp	Olive oil	¼ cup
1 Tbsp	Red wine or Balsamic vinegar	3 Tbsp
3 oz.	Fresh Mozzarella cheese	8 ounces
¼ cup	Fresh basil leaves	¾ cup
¼ tsp	Crushed red pepper	¾ tsp
6 oz.	Penne, or other tubular pasta	1 ½ lb.
2 quart	Saucepan	Dutch oven

1. Slice cherry tomatoes in half. Chop basil and cut mozzarella into bite sized pieces.
2. In a small bowl, mix the tomatoes, olive oil, vinegar, mozzarella cheese, basil and red pepper. Set aside.
3. Cook pasta according to package directions. Drain.
4. Add tomato mixture to drained pasta and toss to mix.

 Serve With:
Sprinkle grated Parmesan cheese and black pepper over each serving if so desired.
Serve with crusty hard rolls and your favorite Chianti.

 Cook's Tip:
Fresh mozzarella can usually be found in the deli section of your local grocery store. If unavailable, substitute Feta, goat cheese or queso fresco.

Pantry Items:
Oil, vinegar, red pepper, pasta

Grocery Items:
Fresh mozzarella, fresh basil, cherry tomatoes,

Time:20 minutes

PASTA SOUP

Sautéing the vermicelli adds a smoky flavor to this Mexican inspired soup.

2 Servings	Ingredients	6 Servings
1 Tbsp	Vegetable oil	2 Tbsp
¾ cup	Vermicelli	2 ¼ cups
1 (10 oz. can)	Red enchilada sauce	3 (10 oz. cans)
2 cups	Beef broth	6 cups
½ cup	Frozen lima beans	1 ½ cups
¼ cup	Cheddar cheese, grated	¾ cup
2 quart	Saucepan	Dutch oven

1. Heat oil in saucepan over medium heat. Break vermicelli into small pieces and add to saucepan.
2. Sauté vermicelli until lightly browned, 2-3 minutes.
3. Add enchilada sauce, beef broth and lima beans to saucepan. Bring to a boil. Reduce heat to medium-low and simmer until pasta is soft, about 8 minutes.
4. Sprinkle each serving with grated cheese.

Pantry Items:
Oil, beef broth, pasta

Grocery Items:
Enchilada sauce, lima beans, cheddar cheese

 Serve With:

Bread sticks, oyster crackers or tortilla chips

109

Time:35 minutes

VEGETABLE SOUP

This is a great way to use up those odds and ends of leftover vegetables in your refrigerator or freezer.

2 Servings	Ingredients	6 Servings
1 small (¾ cup)	Potato	3 small (2 ¼ cups)
2 cups	Vegetable broth	6 cups
¾ cup	Canned tomatoes, cut up	1 (16 oz. can)
¼ cup	Quick cooking barley	¾ cup
1 cup	Frozen mixed vegetables	3 cups
1 tsp	Instant minced onion	1 Tbsp
¼ tsp	Instant minced garlic	¾ tsp
¼ tsp	Dried thyme leaves	½ tsp
¼ tsp	Dried marjoram	¾ tsp
1	Bay Leaf	2
2 quart	Saucepan	Dutch oven

1. Peel and dice potatoes.
2. Add all ingredients to pot.
3. Bring to boil. Reduce heat to medium-low.
4. Cover and cook until potatoes and barley are done, about 20 minutes.
5. Remove bay leaf before serving.

 Serve With:

Sprinkle each serving with grated cheese and serve with rolls.

 Cook's Tip: Rice or small pastas can be used in place of the barley in this recipe.

Pantry Items:
Canned tomatoes, seasonings, broth

Grocery Items:
Barley, potatoes, frozen vegetables.

Time: 45 minutes

CAULIFLOWER CHEESE SOUP

I love thick, creamy soups- but not their high fat content. Here rice thickens the soup instead of butter, with just enough sour cream added to trick your taste buds.

2 Servings	Ingredients	6 Servings
2 large (½ cup)	Carrots	6 large (1 ½ cups)
1 stalk ($^1/_8$ cup)	Celery	3 stalks (1 cup)
1 cup	Cauliflower	3 cups
1 Tbsp	Vegetable oil	3 Tbsp
2 cups	Vegetable broth	6 cups
¼ cup	Uncooked rice	¾ cup
½ cup	Sour cream	1 ½ cups
½ cup	Shredded cheese	1 ½ cups
4 drops	Hot sauce	¼ tsp
2 quart	Saucepan	Dutch oven

1. Chop carrots and celery. Break cauliflower into small pieces. Set aside.
2. Saute carrots and celery in oil over medium heat until soft, 4-5 minutes.
3. Add broth and rice. Bring to boil. Reduce heat to medium-low. Cover and cook for 10-15 more minutes.
4. Add cauliflower pieces. Continue cooking until cauliflower is done, about 10 more minutes.

5. Mix sour cream and cheese. Whisk into soup.
6. Add hot sauce. Serve immediately.

Pantry Items:
Oil, rice, hot sauce, broth

Grocery Items:
Carrots, celery, cauliflower, sour cream, cheese

 Serve With:

Green salad.

 Cook's Tip:

Don't be stingy with the hot sauce. It will enhance the cheese flavor of the soup.

111

Time: 45 minutes

VEGETABLE STEW

Cut the vegetables in smaller pieces to fix this meal even faster.

2 Servings	Ingredients	6 Servings
1 small (¾ cup)	Potato	3 small (2 ¼ cups)
1 large (¼ cup)	Carrots	3 large (¾ cups)
½ large	Bell Pepper	1 large
½ cup.	Fresh mushrooms	1 ½ cups
½ Tbsp	Vegetable oil	1 ½ Tbsp
⅛ cup	Canned tomatoes	1 cup
1 stalk (⅛ cup)	Celery	3 stalks (1 cup)
½ cup	Vegetable broth	1 ½ cup
1 tsp	Instant minced onion	1 Tbsp
½ tsp	Instant minced garlic	1 ½ tsp
1	Bay Leaf	2
¾ cup	Canned garbanzo beans	2 cups
2 quart	Saucepan	Dutch oven

1. Peel potatoes and cut into wedges. Cut bell pepper and carrots in large chunks. Set aside.
2. Heat oil over medium heat. Saute mushrooms until soft, about 5 minutes.
3. Add remaining ingredients. Bring to boil. Reduce heat, cover, and cook for 30 minutes or until vegetables are soft.
4. Remove bay leaf before serving

 Serve with:

Top each serving with plain yogurt.

Pantry Items:
Oil, canned tomatoes, seasonings, broth

Grocery Items:
Mushrooms, potato, carrots, bell pepper, celery

LET'S USE THOSE APPLIANCES

We certainly love our appliances. Look in most American kitchens and you will find a plethora of tools meant to make our lives easier. Here I have included recipes using the most popular, and useful, of those tools; the microwave oven, the slow cooker, the rice cooker, and the newest star of the appliance world, the electric grill Using these appliances will keep the kitchen cool on a hot summer day, or let you have that grilled taste without trudging through the snow in winter to reach the outside gas grill. Need dinner in a real hurry? Make it in the microwave. Have some rice and don't want any other dirty dishes? Let your rice cooker make a complete one-dish meal. Using kitchen appliances does require a little preparation though. Follow these tips and have dinner ready in no time.

♦ Make sure to follow the directions that come with your appliance.

♦ Use potholders when removing dishes from the microwave to avoid nasty burns.

♦ Slow cookers come in many sizes; 2 quart, 4 quart, 6 quart and even larger. The 2 quart size is large enough for 2-4 servings, but use a larger cooker for more than 4 servings.

♦ All recipes here call for a two sided electric grill. If you use a one sided grill, remember to adjust the cooking time.

♦ Meat will not brown when cooked in the microwave. Add sauces for eye-appeal.

♦ Cut meat into small pieces before placing it in the microwave to assure that it cooks completely.

Let's Use Those Appliances

Time: 3 ½ - 10 ½ hours

Slow Cooker

BEEF GOULASH

2 Servings	Ingredients	6 Servings
¾ lb	Stew beef	2 lbs.
2 tsp	Instant minced onion	2 Tbsp
1 tsp	Instant minced garlic	1 ½ tsp
2 tsp	Flour	2 Tbsp
½ tsp	Paprika	1 ½ tsp
1	Bay leaf	1
¼ cup	Beef broth	¾ cup
⅓ cup	Sour cream	1 cup
2 quart	Slow cooker	6 quart

1. Put stew beef, onion, garlic, flour and paprika in slow cooker. Stir to coat meat.
2. Add bay leaf and beef broth. Stir to mix well.
3. Cover and cook on low for 7-10 hours or high for 3-4 hours.
4. Stir in sour cream and cook on low for thirty minutes.
5. Remove bay leaf before serving.

Pantry Items:
Seasonings, flour, broth

Grocery Items:
Stew beef, sour cream

 Serve With:

Hot cooked noodles or rice and steamed brussels sprouts

Time: 2 ½ -9 hours

Slow Cooker

NEW ENGLAND FISH CHOWDER

My first restaurant cooking job was preparing fish chowder for up to 100 every night, and included peeling 50 pounds of potatoes daily. You should find this version easier!

2 Servings	Ingredients	6 Servings
3 slices	Bacon	9 slices
2 large	Potatoes	6 large
¾ lb	Fresh or frozen fish fillets (haddock or cod)	2 ¼ lbs.
2 tsp	Instant minced onion	2 Tbsp
½ cup	Water	1 ½ cups
½ cup	Evaporated milk	1 ½ cups
		1 (13oz. can)
2 quart	Slow Cooker	6 quart

1. Thaw fillets if using frozen fish.
2. Cook bacon in skillet or microwave. Drain and crumble. Place to slow cooker.
3. Peel and dice potatoes. Cut fish fillets into 1 inch pieces.
4. Add potatoes, fish, onion and water to slow cooker.
5. Cover and cook on low for 5-8 hours, or high for 1 ½ to 2 ½ hours.
6. Stir evaporated milk into mixture in slow cooker and continue cooking for one more hour.

Pantry Items:
Dried onion

Grocery Items:
Bacon, potatoes, fish, milk

 **Serve With:**

Oyster crackers

Time: 4-8 hours

Slow Cooker

LAURIE'S THAI CHICKEN

This yummy recipe comes from my friend Laurie, who got it from a friend of hers. Don't be put off by the unusual ingredients. They work together for a fantastic taste treat.

2 Servings	Ingredients	6 Servings
4	Chicken thighs, legs, or breasts	12
½ cup	Medium salsa	1 ½ cups
2 Tbsp	Peanut butter	$\frac{1}{3}$ cup
1 Tbsp	Lemon juice	3 Tbsp
1 ½ tsp	Soy sauce	1 ½ Tbsp
¼ tsp	Ground ginger	¾ tsp
2 quart	Slow cooker	6 quart

1. Remove skin from chicken parts. Rinse chicken and place in slow cooker.
2. Combine salsa, peanut butter, lemon juice, soy sauce and ginger. Spoon over chicken.
3. Cover and cook on low for 7-8 hours, or high for 4-5 hours.

Pantry Items:
Peanut butter, lemon juice, soy sauce, ginger

Grocery Items:
Chicken, salsa

 Serve With:

Rice and a simple spinach salad

Time: 2 -6 hours

Slow Cooker

STEWED GARBANZOS

Garbanzo beans, or chick-peas, are common in Middle Eastern and Indian fare - and American salad bars. They are an tasty, low-fat, high fiber source of protein.

2 Servings	Ingredients	6 Servings
1 large ($^1/_3$ cup)	Carrot	3 (1 cup)
1 cup	Fresh or frozen cauliflower	3 cups
1 (16oz) 2 cups	Canned garbanzo beans, drained and rinsed	3 (16oz) 6 cups
1 tsp	Instant minced onion	1 Tbsp
1 tsp	Instant minced garlic	1 Tbsp
½ tsp	Ground Ginger	1 ¼ tsp
¼ tsp	Turmeric	½ tsp
½ tsp	Sugar	1 ½ tsp
1 cup	Canned tomatoes	3 cups
2 quart	Slow Cooker	6 quart

1. Cut carrot into ½" slices. Separate cauliflower into individual flowerettes if using fresh cauliflower.
2. Add all ingredients to slow cooker. Stir to mix well.
3. Cover and cook on low for 4-6 hours, or high for 2-3 hours.

Pantry Items:
Seasonings, garbanzo beans, canned tomatoes

 Serve With:

Cooked cous cous (see basic recipes). Top with sour cream or plain yogurt.

Grocery Items:
Carrots, cauliflower

118

Time: 4 - 10 hours

Slow Cooker

MARINARA SAUCE

This simple tomato sauce is my very favorite way to enjoy pasta. But if you prefer ragu sauce, add ¼ pound cooked ground beef per serving at step 2.

2 Servings	Ingredients	6 Servings
2 cups	Canned tomatoes	6 cups
1 tsp	Instant minced onion	1 Tbsp
¼ tsp	Crushed red pepper	½ tsp
¼ tsp	Dried basil leaves	½ tsp
1	Bay leaf	1
½ tsp	Salt1	½ tsp.
½ tsp	Brown sugar	1 ½ tsp
1 ½ tsp	Vinegar	1 ½ Tbsp
2 quart	Slow Cooker	6 quart

1. Cut up canned tomatoes. Place in slow cooker.
2. Add all other ingredients. Stir to mix well.
3. Cover and cook on low for 8-10 hours, or high for 4-5 hours.
4. Remove bay leaf before serving.

 Serve With:

Cooked pasta and a green salad

Pantry Items:
Seasonings, salt, brown sugar, vinegar

Grocery Items:
Tomatoes

 Cook's Tip:

If you have frozen, leftover tomato products from other recipes in this book, use in place of the canned tomatoes. It may change the texture of the sauce somewhat, but will still taste delicious.

Time: 4-8 hours

Slow Cooker

MINESTRONE

Top each servings with a spoonful of prepared pesto if desired.

2 Servings	Ingredients	6 Servings
1 cup	Canned navy or cannellini beans	3 cups
2 cups	Beef or vegetable broth	6 cups
1 cup	Frozen mixed vegetables	3 cups
1 cup	Canned tomatoes, diced	3 cups
1 tsp	Instant minced onion	1 Tbsp
½ tsp	Dried basil leaves	1 tsp
1	Bay leaf	1
½ tsp	Instant minced garlic	1 tsp
$\frac{1}{3}$ cup	Small pasta; shells, orzo, or thin noodles	1 cup

1. Drain and rinse beans. Add to slow cooker with broth, vegetables, tomatoes and seasonings.
2. Cover and cook on low for 6 hours, or high for 3 hours.
3. Add pasta and continue cooking for 1-2 hours, or until pasta is al dente. Add more liquid if necessary to prevent burning.
4. Remove bay leaf before serving.

Pantry Items:
Seasonings, pasta, canned tomatoes

Grocery Items:
Canned beans, broth, frozen vegetables

 Serve With:

Italian bread

Time: 20 minutes

Microwave

BEEF AND VEGETABLES

Use any beef cut for this dish. London broil, stew beef, and flank steak all work well.

2 Servings	Ingredients	6 Servings
2 Tbsp	Butter or margarine	⅓ cup
2 Tbsp	Flour	⅓ cup
½ tsp	Dried basil leaves	1 ½ tsp
½ tsp	Dried marjoram	1 tsp
1 tsp	Instant minced onion	1 Tbsp
1 cup	Beef broth	3 cups
½ lb.	Boneless beef	1 ½ lbs.
2 cups	Frozen carrots, green beans mix	6 cups
8 x 8"	Microwave safe baking dish	9 x 13"

1. Melt butter or margarine in the microwave; 30 seconds to 1 minute.
2. Mix flour and seasonings with melted butter. Stir in beef broth.
3. Microwave on high, uncovered, 2 minutes.
4. Meanwhile, cut beef into bite-sized pieces.
5. Stir vegetables and beef pieces into sauce.
6. Microwave for 6 - 8 minutes, or until beef is cooked through.

Pantry Items:
Butter, flour, seasonings, broth

Grocery Items:
Beef, vegetable mix

 Serve With:

Cooked, buttered noodles or baked potato.

Time:25 minutes

Microwave

BEEF CHOW MEIN

Pick up the heat in this dish by adding hot sauce to taste.

2 Servings	Ingredients	6 Servings
½ lb.	Ground beef	1 ½ lbs.
1 tsp	Instant minced onion	1 Tbsp
$\frac{1}{3}$ cup	Beef broth	1 cup
2 tsp	Soy Sauce	2 Tbsp
1 tsp	Sugar	1 Tbsp
1 Tbsp	Flour	3 Tbsp
2 cups	Chow mein vegetables	6 cups
(1 14oz can)		(3 14oz cans)
$\frac{1}{3}$ cup	Canned mushrooms	1 cup
8 x 8"	Microwave safe baking dish	9 x 13"

1. Crumble ground beef into baking dish. Cover with a paper towel. Microwave on high for 2 minutes. Stir to separate.
2. Return to microwave and continue cooking for 2-4 more minutes, or until ground beef is no longer pink.
3. Stir in dried onion, broth, soy sauce, sugar and flour. Mix well. Cover and cook in microwave for 3-6 minutes or until mixture thickens.
4. Stir in drained vegetables and drained mushrooms. Cover and continue cooking an additional 3-5 minutes, or until heated through.

Pantry Items:
Dried onion, broth, soy sauce, sugar, flour

Grocery Items:
Ground beef, chow mein vegetables, mushrooms

 Serve With:
Crisp chow mein noodles or rice.

Time: 25 minutes

Microwave

SUNDAY BRUNCH EGGS AND HAM

Good any day of the week! A strong cheese like Cheddar, Swiss or smoked Gouda is especially good here, but any cheese will work.

2 Servings	Ingredients	6 Servings
1 cup	Frozen, hash brown potatoes	3 cups
1 cup	Cooked ham	3 cups
4	Eggs	12
1 tsp	Instant minced onion	1 Tbsp
2 Tbsp	Milk	6 Tbsp
$\frac{1}{3}$ cup	Shredded cheese	1 cup
8 x 8"	Microwave safe baking dish	9 x 13"

1. Spray baking dish with non-stick spray. Cut ham into bite-sized pieces.
2. Place hash brown potatoes in baking dish. Cover and microwave on high heat, one minute or until partially cooked.
3. Add ham to dish and continue cooking in the microwave for 2 - 4 more minutes, or until mixture is heated.
4. Mix eggs, onion, milk and cheese. Poor over potatoes and ham.
5. Cover baking dish with a splatter guard or paper towel. Microwave for 3 minutes. Stir.
6. Continue cooking for an additional 2 - 6 minutes, or until center is almost set.
7. Let sit for 3-5 minutes before serving.

Pantry Items: Eggs, dried onion, milk

Grocery Items:
Hash brown potatoes, ham, cheese

 Serve With:

Toast or muffins and steamed asparagus.

123

Time: 25 minutes

Microwave

CHICKEN TERIYAKI

2 Servings	Ingredients	6 Servings
2	Frozen, breaded chicken fillets	6
2 Tbsp	Soy sauce	⅓ cup
½ tsp	Ground ginger	1 tsp
1 tsp	Instant minced garlic	2 tsp
1 tsp	Instant minced onion	1 Tbsp
½ tsp	Sugar	1 ½ tsp
¼ cup	Water	¾ cup
2 cups	Frozen, Oriental vegetable mix	6 cups
8 x8"	Microwave safe baking dish	9 x 13"

1. Place frozen chicken fillets in baking dish.
2. Mix soy sauce, ginger, garlic, onion, sugar and water. Pour over chicken. Cover and let sit at room temperature for 15 minutes.
3. Add frozen vegetables to baking dish. Move chicken fillets to top vegetables.
4. Cover with a splatter guard or paper towel. Microwave for 4 - 6 minutes, or until chicken and vegetables are heated through.

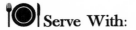 **Serve With:**

White rice

Pantry Items:
Soy sauce, seasonings, sugar

Grocery Items:
Chicken fillets, vegetable mix

Time: 25 minutes

Microwave

CORN CHOWDER

The perfect way to warm your belly on a cold, damp night.

2 Servings	Ingredients	6 Servings
1 Tbsp	Butter or margarine	3 Tbsp
¼ cup	Bell pepper	¾ cup
1 Tbsp	Flour	3 Tbsp
1 ½ tsp	Instant minced onion	1 ½ Tbsp
1 ½ cup	Frozen, hash brown potatoes	4 ½ cups
1 cup	Frozen whole kernel corn	3 cups
1 cup	Chicken broth	3 cups
¾ cup	Milk	2 ¼ cups
dash	Ground red pepper (optional)	½ tsp
medium	Bowl or baking dish	large

1. Chop bell pepper.
2. Melt butter in microwave, 30 seconds. Add chopped bell pepper. Return to microwave and cook on high heat for 2 minutes.
3. Stir in flour and dried onion. Add remaining ingredients and mix well.
4. Cook for 5 minutes. Stir. Continue cooking for 7 - 12 minutes more or until mixture thickens and vegetables are cooked through.
5. Stir in ground red pepper if desired.

Pantry Items:
Butter, flour, dried onion, milk, pepper, broth

Grocery Items:
Bell pepper, hash brown potatoes, corn

 Serve With:

Crackers

Time: 30 minutes

Rice Cooker

ASIAN RICE

Substitute cooked chicken, beef, shrimp or crab for the ham if desired.

2 Servings	Ingredients	6 Servings
¾ cup	Rice	2 ¼ cup
1 ¾ cup	Chicken broth	5 ¼ cup
½ cup	Canned mushrooms	1 ½ cups
½ cup	Cooked ham	1 ½ cups
½ cup	Frozen mixed vegetables	1 ½ cups
1 Tbsp	Soy sauce	3 Tbsp

1. Spray rice bowl with non-stick spray. Drain canned mushrooms.
2. Add all ingredients to rice bowl. Mix well.
3. Cover and start the cooking process.
4. Let sit for 5 minutes after the machine switches to the keep warm cycle.

 Serve With:

Grilled chicken and steamed vegetables.

Pantry Items:
Rice, soy sauce

Grocery Items:
Chicken broth, mushrooms, ham, vegetables

Time: 30 - 50 minutes

Rice Cooker

FISH AND RICE

The steamer cooks the rice while poaching the fish at the same time.

2 Servings	Ingredients	6 Servings
¾ lb.	Fish fillets	2 ¼ lbs.
¾ cup	Rice	2 ¼ cups
2 ¼ cups	Water	6 ¾ cups
½ tsp	Ground ginger	1 tsp
1 tsp	Instant minced onion	1 Tbsp

1. Cut the fish into 2 inch pieces.
2. Spray the rice bowl with non-stick spray.
3. Add the rice, water, ginger and onion to the rice bowl. Stir well.
4. Place fish pieces on top of the rice. Cover and start the cooking process.
5. Let sit 5 minutes after the machine switches to the Keep Warm cycle.

 Serve With:

Steamed green beans and sliced tomatoes.

Pantry Items:
Rice, seasonings

Grocery Items:
Fish fillets

 Cook's Tip:

Place a cup of vinegar near the rice bowl to absorb the smell of the cooking fish.

127

Time: 30 minutes

Rice Cooker

ORANGE CHICKEN AND SPINACH

2 Servings	Ingredients	6 Servings
½ cup	Cooked chicken	1 ½ cups
1 cup	Fresh spinach	3 cups
¾ cup	Rice	2 ¼ cups
¾ cup	Orange juice	2 ¼ cups
1 ½ cups	Chicken broth	4 ½ cups
$^1/_8$ tsp	Crushed red pepper	¼ tsp
1 tsp	Instant minced onion	1 Tbsp

1. Chop the chicken and spinach.
2. Coat the rice bowl with non-stick cooking spray.
3. Add all ingredients to the rice bowl. Mix well.
4. Cover and start the cooking process.
5. Let sit for 5 minutes after the machine switches to the Keep Warm cycle.

Serve With:

Green salad and rolls.

Pantry Items:
Rice, seasonings, broth

Grocery Items:
Chicken, spinach, orange juice

Time: 35 - 40 minutes

Rice Cooker

RED BEANS AND RICE

A quick and easy take on a southern favorite.

2 Servings	Ingredients	6 Servings
¼ cup	Bell pepper	¾ cup
1 cup	Canned kidney beans	3 cups
(8 oz can)		(1 ½ 16 oz cans)
1 ½ cups	Chicken broth	4 ½ cups
½ cup	White or brown rice	1 ½ cups
1 tsp	Instant minced onion onion	1 Tbsp
2 Tbsp	Crumbled bacon or bacon bits	$\frac{1}{3}$ cup
	(optional)	

1. Spray rice bowl with non-stick spray.
2. Chop bell pepper. Drain and rinse kidney beans.
3. Add all ingredients to rice bowl. Stir well and start the cooking process.
4. Let sit for 5 minutes after the machine switches to the Keep Warm cycle.
5. Top with salt, pepper, chopped tomato and shredded cheese if desired.

Pantry Items:
Rice, dried onion, broth

Grocery Items:
Bell pepper, kidney beans, bacon

 Serve With:

Green salad or steamed greens.

129

Time:45 - 50 minutes

Rice Cooker

THE THREE B'S

Barley, brown rice, and broccoli - a great source of minerals and an tasty way to eat more grains.

2 Servings	Ingredients	6 Servings
¼ cup	Red or orange bell pepper	¾ cup
¼ cup	Quick cooking barley	¾ cup
½ cup	Brown rice	1 ½ cups
2 ½ cups	Vegetable broth	7 ½ cups
1 tsp	Dried marjoram	2 tsp
½ cup	Frozen chopped broccoli	1 ½ cup

1. Spray rice bowl with non-stick cooking spray. Chop bell pepper.
2. Add bell pepper, barley, rice, broth and marjoram to the rice bowl. Mix well.
3. Cover and start the cooking process. Cook for 20 minutes.
4. Add frozen broccoli to rice bowl. Stir. Cover and continue cooking until done.
5. Let sit for 5 minutes after the machine switches to the Keep Warm cycle.

 Serve With:

Grilled chicken or burgers.

 Cook's Tip: You can find quick cooking barley at your grocers or health food store. If you want to use pearled barley instead, soak it in cold water for one hour before adding to the rice cooker.

Pantry Items:
Marjoram, brown rice, broth

Grocery Items:
Barley, frozen broccoli, pimento

Time:15 - 30 minutes

Electric Grill

EVERYDAY BURGERS

Burgers are quick, easy, and even the kids will eat them. And by using your indoor grill, there's no time wasted waiting for the charcoal to be ready.

2 Servings	Ingredients	6 Servings
½ lb	Ground beef	1 ½ lbs.
²/₃ cup	Bread crumbs or oatmeal	1 cup
1	Egg	1
1 tsp	Instant minced onion	1 Tbsp
1 Tbsp	Prepared mustard	3 Tbsp

1. Preheat the grill to its warmest setting.
2. In a large bowl, mix all ingredients together. Shape into burgers no thicker than 3/4 inch.
3. Grill for 10 - 20 minutes or until juices run clear.

Pantry Items:
Bread crumbs, egg, onion, mustard

Grocery Items:
Ground beef

 Serve With:

Sliced tomato, pickle and sesame seed hamburger buns.

 Cook's Tip: Use spicy mustard for added hamburger zing.

131

Time: 20 - 30 minutes

Electric Grill

EVERYDAY STEAKS

Use London broil, New York strip, or flank steaks.

2 Servings	Ingredients	6 Servings
2 small	Boneless beef steaks	6 small
1 tsp	Lemon-pepper seasoning	1 Tbsp
½ tsp	Salt1	½ tsp

1. Preheat grill to highest setting.
2. Wash steaks and pat dry with a paper towel.
3. Rub the steaks with the lemon pepper and salt.
4. Grill until steaks have reached desired cooking stage, approximately 8 minutes for rare, 9 minutes for medium, 10 minutes for well done.

 Serve With:

Baked potato, corn on the cob and sliced tomato.

Pantry Items:
Seasonings

Grocery Items:
Steak

Time:40 minutes

Electric Grill

MARINATED TUNA STEAKS

Extra-virgin olive oil adds flavor to this marinade, but other cooking oils can be successfully used too.

2 Servings	Ingredients	6 Servings
1 tsp	Dried basil leaves	1 Tbsp
1 tsp	Instant minced garlic	1 Tbsp
2 Tbsp	Lemon juice	$\frac{1}{3}$ cup
2 Tbsp	Vegetable oil	$\frac{1}{3}$ cup
¾ lb.	Tuna steaks	2 ¼ lbs.

1. Combine basil, garlic, lemon juice and cooking oil to make marinade.
2. Rinse the fish and pat dry with a paper towel. Cut into smaller pieces if necessary to fit on grill.
3. Put fish in a plastic zipper bag. Add marinade. Let sit for 20 minutes to 1 hour.
4. When ready to cook, preheat grill to medium high setting (about 5 minutes).
5. Discard marinade. Place tuna steaks on grill and cook for 5-10 minutes, or until done as desired.

Pantry Items:
Seasonings, lemon juice, oil

Grocery Items:
Tuna steaks

 Serve With:

Green salad and rice pilaf.

133

Time:25 - 45 minutes

Electric Grill

GRILLED APRICOT TURKEY

Chicken breasts can be used in place of the turkey tenderloins.

2 Servings	Ingredients	6 Servings
¼ cup	Apricot jam or preserves	$^2/_3$ cup
2 Tbsp	Orange juice	$^1/_3$ cup
2 Tbsp	Prepared mustard	$^1/_3$ cup
1 tsp	Dried marjoram	2 tsp
2	Boneless turkey breast tenderloins	6

1. Spray grill with non-stick cooking spray. Preheat to highest setting.
2. Combine apricot jam, orange juice, mustard and marjoram.
3. Wash turkey breasts and pat dry with a paper towel.
4. Brush turkey breasts with the jam mixture.
5. Cook for 5 minutes. Turn and brush with jam mixture. Cook for an additional 5 - 7 minutes, or until meat is no longer pink.

 Serve With:

Cooked, buttered noodles and peas and carrots.

Pantry Items:
Mustard, marjoram

Grocery Items:
Apricot jam, orange juice, turkey breast tenderloins

Time: 35 minutes

Electric Grill

GARLIC-ROSEMARY CHICKEN

Rosemary is an herb often used in Mediterranean cooking. It provides a deep, earthy taste especially good with meats.

2 Servings	Ingredients	6 Servings
1 tsp	Instant minced garlic	1 Tbsp
1 tsp	Dried rosemary	2 tsp
2 Tbsp	Vegetable oil	$1/_3$ cup
2 Tbsp	Lemon juice	$1/_3$ cup
2	Boneless, skinless chicken breasts	6

1. Combine the garlic, rosemary, oil and lemon juice.
2. Wash the chicken breasts and pat dry with a paper towel.
3. Place chicken in a plastic, zippered bag. Add marinade. Set aside for 20 minutes to 1 hour.
4. When ready to cook, preheat grill to highest setting.
5. Discard marinade. Grill chicken breasts for 8-9 minutes, or until juices are clear.

 Serve With:

Baked potato and steamed brussels sprouts. Or serve with sliced tomato and mayonnaise in a toasted sandwich bun.

Pantry Items:
Dried garlic, oil, lemon juice

Grocery Items:
Dried rosemary, chicken

135

Time: 20 minutes

Electric Grill

VEGETABLE QUESADILLAS

This is a great mixture to keep on hand in the refrigerator. Then when your teens get home from soccer practice they can easily make their own nutritious meal. Top each quesadilla with plain yogurt and salsa.

2 Servings	Ingredients	6 Servings
½ cup	Canned pinto or black beans	1 ½ cups
½ cup	Frozen whole kernel corn	1 ½ cups
⅓ cup	Tomato	1 cup
1 Tbsp	Canned, diced green chiles	3 Tbsp
¾ cup	Monterey jack cheese, shredded	2 ¼ cups
½ tsp	Chili powder	½ tsp
4	Flour tortillas	12

1. Preheat grill to medium-high setting.
2. Drain and rinse beans. Run corn under hot water to thaw. Chop tomato.
3. In a large bowl, combine corn, beans, chilis, tomato, cheese, and chili powder.
4. Divide mixture among half of the tortillas, about ¾ cup each. Top with remaining tortillas.
5. Gently transfer quesadillas to grill, and cook for 5-7 minutes. Let sit for 1 minute before serving.

Pantry Items:
None

 Serve With:

Mexican rice and steamed zucchini

Grocery Items:
Corn, beans, chiles, tomato, cheese, tortillas

Time: 20 minutes

Electric Grill

VEGETARIAN BURGERS

The perfect way to add grains to your diet. You won't even miss the meat.

2 Servings	Ingredients	6 Servings
¼ cup	Quick cooking rice (brown or white)	¾ cup
¼ cup	Quick oatmeal	¾ cup
¼ cup	Bread crumbs	¾ cup
2 Tbsp	Peanut butter	$\frac{1}{3}$ cup
¼ cup	Cottage cheese	¾ cup
1 tsp	Instant minced onion	1 Tbsp
1 tsp	Instant minced garlic	1 Tbsp
½ tsp	Dried basil leaves	1 ½ tsp

1. Mix rice and oatmeal in a large bowl. Pour boiling water over mixture. Cover bowl and let sit for 5 minutes.
2. Preheat grill to highest setting.
3. Drain rice/oatmeal mixture. Add bread crumbs, peanut butter, cottage cheese, onion, garlic and bail. Mix well. Shape into burgers, approximately ¾ inch thick.
4. Grill for 6 - 8 minutes, or until browned. Gently remove from grill.

Pantry Items:
Rice, bread crumbs, peanut butter, seasonings

Grocery Items:
Oatmeal, cottage cheese

 Serve With:

Pepper Jack cheese, sliced tomato and onion, and sesame seed hamburger buns.

137

NUTRITION AND HEALTH

Eating a variety of foods, along with plenty of exercise, will keep your body healthy and strong. Make sure your meals include the following every day.

- **Carbohydrates:** Provide the body with energy. Good sources include rice, pasta, fruits and vegetables.

- **Protein:** Essential for growth and repair. Good sources include meats, fish, dairy products, beans and nuts.

- **Fats:** Useful for long term energy and help protect the nervous system, but only needed in very limited amounts. Good sources are oils and seeds.

- **Vitamins:** Help other nutrients do their work. There are many different vitamins. Good sources include fresh fruits and vegetables, milk, and cereals.

- **Minerals:** Also needed to help the other nutrients do their work. Sources of major minerals are dairy products, legumes, fish and seafood, fruits and vegetables.

- **Water:** Needed to bring every cell in your body the nutrients it needs. You should drink 6 to 8 cups of water per day.

WEEKLY MENU

Now there is an answer to "what's for dinner tonight?" The following will keep you organized and eliminate one more daily task. The menus are designed with variety in mind. The very easiest dishes are toward the end of the week, a time when many of us lack the energy to cook elaborate meals. They are also arranged to streamline grocery shopping. For example, if you use ½ can of soup in a recipe early in the week, later that week is another recipe using the other half can. Follow this daily plan and you will be the envy of the office - because you know "what's for dinner tonight", and tomorrow night, and the next night, and the next.................

Index

143